SANSINUKUBAN is the official book series of the Ateneo de Davao University International Studies Department. It serves as a platform for students to publish original research articles primarily derived from their thesis and inspired by their Mindanao positionality. The book aims to foster vibrant scholarly dialogue among them and seeks to promote interdisciplinary approaches to critically analyze the intricacies and conundrums of our diverse and complex world.

SANSINUKUBAN 1
INTERNATIONAL STUDIES FROM MINDANAO

Traversing Spatial and Ideational Frontiers

Edited by

Jaecian Onoh A. Cesar
Justine Christie C. Buhia
Pola Gabrielle E. Cuadrillero
Christabel Erica L. Nicolas

SANSINUKUBAN 1: International Studies from Mindanao
Traversing Spatial and Ideational Frontiers

EDITORS
Jaecian Onoh A. Cesar
Justine Christie C. Buhia
Pola Gabrielle E. Cuadrillero
Christabel Erica L. Nicolas

BOARD OF REVIEWERS
John Harvey D. Gamas, MA, *International Studies Department*
Maria Lourdes S. Braceros, MSc, *International Studies Department*
Krizza Janica B. Mahinay, MA, *International Studies Department*
Monica A. Villa Abrille, MAS, *International Studies Department*
Rhisan Mae E. Morales, MA, *International Studies Department*
Jose Enrique C. Sibala, MILIR, *International Studies Department*
Rhodalie O. Emilio, MPA, *Political Science and History Department*
Mansoor L. Limba, PhD, *Islamic Studies Department*

ISBN 9798326309235

Published by ElziStyle Bookshop
Email: admin@elzistyle.com
Website: www.elzistyle.com

COVER ARTIST
Danika Maria Sandra B. Corias

CONTENTS

Introduction

The Editors

We live in a world constantly pushed at the throes of societal change marked by superpower rivalries, economic booms and busts, transnational migrations, inter-state conflicts, civil strife, and health and environmental catastrophes. It is precisely this enduring dynamism of the international system that challenges us students of International Studies to rise above the traditional canons of our discipline and delve deeper into the pursuit for universality—our *sansinukuban*. Indeed, the turbulent waters we are now in unmasks the reality that much is to be desired beyond the dominant Western paradigms that have long colored our lenses about the world. Crucially, the pursuit for such a universality begins when we interrogate spatial and ideational contexts that have dictated our understanding of the "international."

The currency of power and its attendant abuse relied heavily on what and whose *ideas* prevailed. The constructions and politics of *space* have also defined who gets to occupy our world's physical and abstract spaces. Such understandings about *ideas* and *space* revealed that exclusivity and barriers have only led to the crises of (mis)representations that resonate in our present zeitgeist. While not necessarily disregarding the time-honored insights conferred by the realist, liberal, and constructivist frameworks, a pivot towards universality in International Studies allows us to engage with the eclectic and unconventional notions about the spatial and ideational relations from the peripheries. Therefore, the deep and abiding Eurocentrism of our discipline call us aspiring scholars of the Ateneo de Davao to take part in the non-Western project of universalizing the diversity of epistemologies. On this maiden issue of Sansinukuban, we seek to open up academic space for voices in the margins, reflect on our Mindanawon positionalities, and challenge the artificial divide between the local and the international.

The studies present in this book, ranging from analyses of

immigrant securitization efforts and mapping of public diplomacy initiatives to the post- and de-colonial constructions of sports cultures and sub-regional trade, reflect the intersectionality of the spatial contexts and ideational underpinnings of our world today.

In illuminating the power of food in generating new ideas and mindsets, as well as in carving a nation's space in the diplomatic milieu, the first chapter presents the evolving awareness of engaging diverse international audiences in gastrodiplomacy strategies, a new form of soft power state actors can tap or leverage. Buhia, Bugnos, Diligencia, Sario, and Tumala's study draws attention to the Philippines' increasing engagement in its food-related initiatives, signaling a shift from relative obscurity to a noticeable enterprise in leveraging soft power internationally.

The study of Cesar, Corias, Jusa, and Magallanes in the second chapter aims to spotlight the non-West's agency on subverting and accomodating Western hegemonic impulses by analyzing Philippine basketball culture vis-a-vis American basketball. More importantly, their study illuminates how the Filipinos have appropriated the American-dominated sport with local techniques, narratives, and values, revealing the non-West's volition to consciously adapt and retool hegemonic cultural influences to empower themselves and reassert their space in a Western-led sporting arena.

In the third chapter, Dagala, Cuadrillero, Kimamao, Señas, and Yap's research engages with the non-Western traditions of International Relations by addressing the enduring Western paradigms that had stymied the BIMP-EAGA's integration efforts. Their study unraveled the prevailing colonial paradigms that implicitly imposes a Western-modeled approach to integration and which ultimately hampers the economic growth of the sub-region.

In the final chapter, Nicolas, Lomogdang, and Esteron's study centers the discourse on physical spaces, particularly in the context of the immigrant deportation regime in the United States. Their study deconstructs the immigrant American dream by dissecting how the Obama administration's securitization efforts shaped the politics and the conceptual space of those who truly "belong."

Sansinukuban seeks to bring forth more nuanced perspectives on the spatial and ideational frontiers of International Studies. May this book and its subsequent volumes contribute to the nudging of those barriers circumscribed by a handful of Western epistemologies and ultimately widen our pathways toward an academic terrain no longer constricted within a homogenizing worldview.

Chapter 1

The Filipino Flavor Trail: Mapping the Components of Philippine Gastrodiplomacy, 2015-2022*

Justine Christie C. Buhia, Jieyeen Grace E. Bugnos,
Katrina Andrea D. Diligencia, Skye Danielle N. Sario, &
Kim Vincent D. Tumala

ABSTRACT

Gastrodiplomacy is public diplomacy employed by state and non-state actors in their food-related initiatives to foster positive foreign relations in pursuit of political, economic, and social benefits. While the Philippines has actively engaged in gastrodiplomacy since 2015 with increased state and non-state participation, there remains an unstructured and disconnected understanding of Philippine gastrodiplomacy, constraining its potential to maximize its benefits. This research sought to map Philippine gastrodiplomacy from 2015 to 2022 by identifying its fundamental components: the actors conducting Philippine gastrodiplomacy, their process of generating influence, and the resulting new mindsets. In this qualitative study, the researchers used Aigerim Raimzhanova's Soft Power Resources and Lee Geun's Stages of Conversion. The findings of the study revealed the two categories of Philippine gastrodiplomacy's agents: primary agents, comprising state and non-state actors forming the core driving force, and supplementary agents, including government agencies, international cultural associations, public culinary personalities and restaurateurs, and business and corporations. The agents generated influence by expanding their network resources through exclusive and inclusive collaboration while selecting a limited number of long-term initiatives and high-yield one-time initiatives. As a result, the Philippines is viewed as an emerging culinary destination with diverse yet underutilized culinary resources and a source of diasporic identity and profession. Based on these results, the researchers concluded that Philippine gastrodiplomacy is pursued more as a strategy than an institutionalized system, with its decentralized, unconcerted, and unsustained conduct.

Keywords: *Gastrodiplomacy, Soft power, Cultural diplomacy, Philippines*

---

*Awarded as Best Thesis
for AB International Studies Major in Asian Studies (2024).

Introduction

Soft power refers to a state's ability to influence others' behaviors and perceptions toward shared objectives using non-coercive strategies (Nye, 2008; Lee, 2009). This strength relies on intangible assets such as political institutions, culture, and policies, as well as the perception of legitimacy by recipients (Lee, 2009; Raimzhanova, 2015). Gastrodiplomacy, involving food-related initiatives by both state and non-state actors, is an example of using soft power to cultivate national brands through culinary diplomacy (Awang & Nirwandy, 2014; Rockower, 2012). The term was coined in response to Thailand's 'Kitchen to the World' public diplomacy campaign to enhance the nation's brand, tourism, and food exports, thereby deepening foreign relations (Pornpongmeta, 2019; Rockower, 2012).

Gastrodiplomacy is characterized by the harmonization of active stakeholder engagement, ample resources, and a well-defined strategy. However, mere presence, as seen in Indonesia's case,

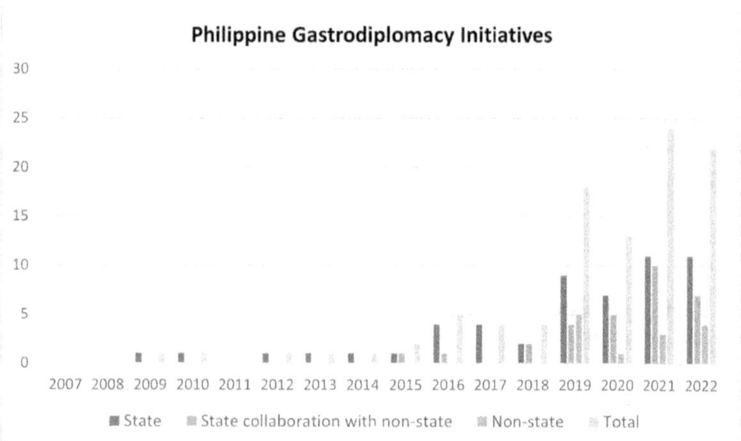

Figure 1. *Philippine Gastrodiplomacy Initiatives*

does not ensure success, necessitating the harmonization of all elements for consistent and sustainable gastrodiplomacy. Similar to neighboring countries, the Philippines has long been engaged in gastrodiplomacy, with recent initiatives showing a notable surge and highlighting the country's proactive gastrodiplomacy approach to engaging target audiences. Figure 1 illustrates the frequency of gastrodiplomacy initiatives in the Philippines from 2007 to 2022, highlighting two distinct periods: 2007-2014, characterized by low visibility gastrodiplomacy, and 2015-2022, marked by heightened visibility. Researchers compiled this data by analyzing reports and articles from various government and news sources.

The years 2007-2014 saw only five events that were state-led but used non-state actors as contributors. The events' nature saw little public participation; instead, state actors appealed to VIPs, which is the norm in traditional diplomacy (Embassy of the Philippines Tokyo, Japan, 2009a, 2010b, 2014c; Official Gazette, 2012). This is opposed to gastrodiplomacy since it leans towards public diplomacy. The sparse number and prevalence of state actors signify how little return could be generated by conducting gastrodiplomacy at this time, thus explaining its low visibility status. Meanwhile, the years 2015-2018 saw sixteen events. The Philippine government, through numerous agencies, began various projects such as thematic food festivals overseas, printing cookbooks for foreign audiences, and participating in foreign expos and fairs. These efforts also involved hosting events in the Philippines and increasing collaboration with non-state actors to participate and assist in their programs (Department of Foreign Affairs, 2015, 2016, 2017a; Diplomat Magazine, 2017; Mellejor, 2018).

During 2019-2022, Philippine gastrodiplomacy initiatives increased, totaling more than fifty, with increased coverage of independent activity by non-state actors. This period marked a growing state-wide promotional campaign targeting high-profile state and non-state actors, enhanced partnerships with other states through bodies like BIMP-EAGA, and increased assertiveness from non-state actors promoting Philippine cuisine internationally (Daza-Puyat, 2019; Department of Foreign Affairs, 2019a, 2019b). This upward trend faced setbacks in 2020 because of COVID-19, as events and projects were canceled or postponed. The Philippines adapted to this circumstance by digitizing its campaigns and events (Department of Foreign Affairs, 2020a, 2020b, 2020c, 2020d, 2020e). By 2021-2022, the number of assessed initiatives increased to a combined total of forty-six, as collaborations began to equal the number of state-led events as Philippine gastrodiplomacy extended its reach to foreign audiences with the widespread use of social media and the internet (Asiddao, n.d.; Cruz, 2022). Additionally, during 2021-2022, Representative Loren Legarda introduced House Bill No. 10551 and Senate Bill No. 244, which aimed at general education, collaboration with relevant stakeholders, and the establishment of a committee to oversee these efforts (An Act Providing for the Development and Preservation of Philippine Culinary Heritage, 2021; Philippine Gastronomy and Culinary Heritage Development Act, 2022). Additionally, House Bill No. 619, which was introduced by another representative, contains similar provisions (Philippine Gastronomy and Culinary Heritage Development Act, 2022). While primarily focused on domestic matters, one provision of these bills mentioned the inclusion of gastrodiplomacy under the jurisdiction of the Department of Foreign Affairs (DFA), suggesting their potential role in directing national gastrodiplomacy, albeit without specific details.

The surge in the Philippines' gastrodiplomacy activities marks a significant advancement in the nation's soft power potential. Before 2015, limited visibility resulted from various factors: shifts in government focus, high operational costs, inadequate global availability of Filipino ingredients, and insufficient culinary recognition. Post-2015, heightened visibility, with over seventy-nine initiatives, including thirty collaborations, reflects contrasting factors like the Duterte administration's emphasis on gastrodiplomacy, cost reductions due to global trade partnerships, rising Filipino diaspora nationalism, and increased non-state involvement. These intersecting factors have shaped the trajectory of Philippine gastrodiplomacy, illuminating its evolution and potential impact on global perceptions of Filipino cuisine and culture.

The scholarly literature on Philippine gastrodiplomacy high-lighted Filipino culinary tourism as a key driver for attracting local and foreign tourism, emphasizing the significance of food in the tourism sector. However, there is a notable gap in the comprehensive exploration of Philippine gastrodiplomacy's specific components and a lack of consensus among actors regarding its definition. While the Philippines has actively engaged in gastrodiplomacy since 2015 with increased state and non-state participation, there remains an unstructured and disconnected understanding of Philippine gastrodiplomacy, constraining its potential to maximize its benefits and compete effectively with its neighbors. Thus, the primary purpose of this study is to map Philippine gastrodiplomacy from 2015-2022 to provide a comprehensive understanding of its components. Specifically, the researchers aimed to identify the state and non-state actors involved in Philippine gastrodiplomacy, examine the actors' mechanisms to generate influence and attraction, and explore the emerging mindset about the Philippines resulting from their gastrodiplomacy initiatives.

The researchers employed the case study approach to analyze Philippine gastrodiplomacy from 2015 to 2022. The primary data sources included first-hand accounts, reports, and opinions from state actors [Department of Foreign Affairs (DFA), Department of Tourism (DOT), Department of Trade and Industry (DTI), Department of Agriculture (DA)], non-state actors (Filipino Food Movement Australia, Mama Sita's, Kulinarya Qatar), and non-state individuals involved in Philippine gastrodiplomacy. The secondary sources used for data collection were scholarly articles, journals, and books. The researchers used purposive and snowball sampling to select the respondents and collected the data through online interviews and written correspondence. Afterwards, the researchers analyzed the data using Raimzhanova's (2015) Soft Power Resources and Lee's (2009) Stages of Conversion. While the study did not directly involve the recipients of Philippine gastrodiplomacy, the feedback outputs that the state and non-state actors could gather from their recipients were examined and corroborated with published data.

Raimzhanova's Soft Power Resources and Lee's Stages of Conversion

This study is anchored on Aigerim Raimzhanova's (2015) *Soft Power Resources* and Lee Geun's (2009) *Stages of Conversion of Soft Resources into Soft Power*. Raimzhanova's (2015) theory precisely categorizes *soft power resources*, which are the elements that produce attraction (Nye, 2008, p. 95). The first soft power resource is *Agents*, encompassing individuals and entities that create and implement soft power initiatives (Raimzhanova, 2015, p. 9). *Agents* comprise a range of actors who implement soft power initiatives, including nation-states, non-governmental organizations, multinational corporations, and individuals (Raimzhanova, 2015, p. 10). The second soft power resource is *Spheres*, which refers to the areas in which soft power is derived (Raimzhanova, 2015, p. 9). Different *spheres* include "foreign politics, domestic politics, culture & history, education & science, business, creative industries, technologies, tourism, sport, and environment" (Raimzhanova, 2015, p. 9). The third soft power resource is *Instruments*, which entails the specific vehicles, methods, or tools that activate soft power (Raimzhanova, 2015, p. 9). Such *instruments* may include programs, initiatives, events, conferences, and laws that allow agents to exercise soft power to their recipients. Raimzhanova visualizes the relationship between the *soft power resources* as interdependent (Raimzhanova, 2015, p. 10), of which the effectiveness of a certain soft power resource relies on the utilization of the other elements. In the context of Philippine gastrodiplomacy, this theory can assist in identifying the components that form the basis of soft power.

Raimzhanova also highlights the importance of consistent and adequate resource utilization for such initiatives to be effective, emphasizing two key factors essential for achieving lasting impacts: *scale and sustainability* (Raimzhanova, 2015, p. 12, 15). *Scale* refers to the extent of proponents involved and the extent of institutional support in implementing soft power initiatives (Raimzhanova, 2015, p. 12). Meanwhile, *sustainability* involves consistently utilizing soft power resources to achieve the long-term goals of soft power, such as a lasting influence on its recipients (Raimzhanova, 2015, p. 12-13). In the context of Philippine gastrodiplomacy, Raimzhanova's *scale and sustainability* can be utilized to assess the influence of its gastrodiplomacy programs.

Furthermore, Lee's *Stages of Conversion* (2009) explains the conversion of soft power resources to soft power through a three-stage process. The first stage is the *application of soft power resources*, which refers to using symbolic resources by state and non-state actors in the area in which they operate (Lee, 2009, p. 209). However, Lee argues that having access to soft power resources does not automatically generate soft power. This means that soft power has not yet been produced at this stage, as the intention of generating influence using such resources has not yet been realized. The second stage is *co-optive* or *soft power production*, which entails the production of attraction and influence (Lee, 2009, p. 210). This stage involves converting the actors' soft power resources into soft power, wherein the applicant's objective of generating influence in the first stage is realized. The third stage is the creation of a *new interpretative framework*, which refers to the soft power recipients' production of patterned, continuous thinking and behavior due to the agents' constant application of co-optive power (Lee, 2009, p. 211). The recipients of soft power include foreign mass audiences, elites, and the Filipino diaspora abroad. According to Lee, producing a *new interpretative framework* for receivers is the objective of soft power projection for the applicant to effect substantial and long-term change (Lee, 2009, p. 211).

The researchers used the first stage to identify the state and non-state actors involved in Philippine gastrodiplomacy. The second stage was also used to determine how state actors generated soft power from soft power resources. Meanwhile, the third stage was utilized to examine the *new interpretative framework* generated from soft power projection.

Actors of Philippine Gastrodiplomacy

Philippine gastrodiplomacy operates through a dynamic interplay of primary and supplementary agents. The primary agents, the core driving forces, are state and non-state actors. These agents and supplementary actors, like government bodies, cultural associations, culinary personalities, and businesses, work together to execute gastrodiplomacy initiatives (Raimzhanova, 2015). They promote Filipino cuisine, foster cultural understanding, and enhance international relations through various instruments like festivals, cooking shows, and online campaigns, among many others.

In Philippine gastrodiplomacy, primary agents are subdivided into state and non-state actors. Primary agents, identified by their institutional mandates, significant resources, and extensive networks, play a vital role in promoting the nation's culinary heritage and fostering cultural understanding. Notably, they possess substantial resources and a broader reach than supplementary agents, benefiting from institutional networks that facilitate strategic resource deployment.

First, the Department of Tourism (DOT), operating within the tourism sphere, utilizes various instruments like festivals and expos in Philippine gastrodiplomacy to promote tourism as a significant socio-economic activity (Department of Tourism, n.d). An example of their initiatives is the *2023 National Tourism Development Plan* (NTDP), which underscored Food and Gastronomy as a pivotal component, reflecting a shift since 2016 towards emphasizing the nation's culinary traditions (Rocamora, 2018). This refocus included developing "culinary tourism," which was evident in events like the *Madrid Fusion Culinary Event* in Manila in 2018 (Castro, personal communication, 2023).

Second, the National Commission for Culture and the Arts (NCCA) is crucial in promoting Filipino cuisine within the cultural sphere through food exhibitions and symposiums (National Commission for Culture and the Arts, n.d.). As the national state agency for arts and culture, the NCCA administers the National Endowment Fund for Culture and the Arts (NEFCA) and executes initiatives like *Filipino Food Month* and *Sentro Rizal* to promote Philippine culture globally. For instance, *Sentro Rizal* organized the *Linamnam: A Philippine Culinary Heritage and Gastronomy*

Symposium in collaboration with the Philippine Culinary Heritage Movement, featuring presentations by Filipino food historian Ms. Felice Prudente Sta. Maria and cooking demonstrations by celebrity chef Myke "Tatung" Sarthou (Embassy of the Philippines Canberra, Australia, 2021). These efforts promoted Filipino culinary traditions while reconnecting Filipinos abroad, especially migrant children, with their cultural roots (Embassy of the Philippines Canberra, Australia, 2021).

Third, the Department of Foreign Affairs (DFA), whose mandates encompass national security, economic welfare, and cultural diplomacy, operates within cultural and foreign political spheres (Department of Foreign Affairs n.d.; Philippine Embassy of Qatar, personal communication, October 9, 2023). Gastrodiplomacy initiatives, aligned with the DFA's fourth pillar, utilize various instruments like festivals, food months, and bazaars. For instance, the Philippine Embassy in Amman, Jordan, organized the *Annual Diplomatic Bazaar* in 2015, where the Embassy showcased traditional Filipino handicrafts, accessories, textiles, and souvenirs, along with native delicacies such as *polvoron, sago't gulaman,* dried mangoes, and more. The Embassy also distributed Philippine tourism brochures and displayed *'It's More Fun in the Philippines'* posters, inviting visitors to explore the country (DFA Jordan, 2015 ; DFA, Republic of the Philippines, 2015). Besides this, the DFA's Office of Public and Cultural Diplomacy (OPCD) also directs initiatives such as *Filipino Food Month* and Independence Day celebrations (Philippine Embassy in Qatar, personal communication, October 9, 2023).

Non-state actors like the Filipino Food Movement (FFM), Mama Sita's, Kulinarya Qatar, and individuals such as Ige Ramos and Clang Garcia also play vital roles in Philippine gastrodiplomacy. They promote Filipino cuisine through various cultural, business, and tourism initiatives, including establishing restaurants, organizing festivals, and collaborating with stakeholders (Filipino Food Movement, n.d.; Filipino Food Movement Australia, n.d.).

Mama Sita's is unique because it encompasses its business

arm, the Mama Sita's Holding Company, and its non-profit organization, Mama Sita's Foundation. Regardless of the division, both entities promote Philippine culinary heritage and traditions while engaging in business by selling food products (Mama Sita's, n.d.; Mama Sita's Foundation, n.d.). Ultimately, both arms exert influence in business and culture.

Kulinarya Qatar, a cultural movement formed in Qatar in 2015 by Filipino restaurateurs and supported by the Philippine Embassy in Doha, aims to promote Filipino cuisine within Filipino and non-Filipino communities (Philippine Embassy in Doha, Qatar, personal communication, October 9, 2023). Over the years, it has grown more independent and expanded its scope, organizing annual events like the *Food, Culture, and Trade Festival* in collaboration with the Philippine Embassy in Doha and celebrity chefs (Regis, 2023; Tunay, 2022). According to Ms. Dahlia Agbanlog, the chairperson of Kulinarya Qatar, their initiatives include various festivals and events such as the *Filipino Food Festival, Filipino Community Family Day*, and *Fiesta ng Kalayaan* (Agbanlog, personal communication, October 10, 2023).

Individuals such as Clang Garcia are also significant players in Philippine gastrodiplomacy, making substantial contributions beyond academic research. Garcia, a Filipino food scholar, specializes in product and destination development, immersive travel experiences, and educational content across various media platforms (Garcia, personal communication, September 22, 2023). She lobbied for *Filipino Food Month*, which President Duterte signed into effect. She also authored a book entitled "Philippine Food Holidays," detailing her experiences in engaging with notable figures in gastronomy amidst the pandemic.

Another primary agent in the field of Philippine gastrodiplomacy is Ige Ramos. Known for his roles as a food writer and book designer, Ramos has made significant contributions to the world of food and culture (Ramos, personal communication, September 27, 2023). Recognized as one of Asia's Most Influential Figures in the realm of Food and Beverage by Philippine Tattler's Tastemakers in 2021, Ramos's commitment to culinary heritage and the *Slow Food Movement* is evident through his active involvement with Slow Food and the Philippine Culinary Heritage Movement.

Supplementary agents in Philippine gastrodiplomacy, categorized into four groups, contribute diverse strengths to enhance the country's culinary and cultural identity worldwide. Governmental agencies preserve culinary heritage, while cultural associations foster appreciation abroad. Culinary personalities act as ambassadors, and businesses support gastrodiplomacy through partnerships. Government agencies play a vital role in gastrodiplomacy, despite their primary mandates not exclusively focusing on food, as they are tasked with attracting foreign investments, fostering trade relations, and promoting various sectors of the Philippine economy.

The Department of Agriculture (DA) promotes agricultural development through events like food expositions and festivals (Department of Agriculture, n.d.). Mr. Canceran, a Planning Officer at the Philippine Rural Development Project, highlights the DA's role in the food value chain, emphasizing production and post-harvest activities (D. Canceran, personal communication, October 9, 2023). The DA leads *Filipino Food Month* and collaborates with organizations like the World Food Expo for gastrodiplomacy efforts (Vergara, 2023; Sicat, 2023). Meanwhile, the Department of Trade and Industry (DTI) utilizes trade promotion programs and exhibitions with investment forums and conferences within the business sphere. Affiliated agencies like the Center for International Trade Expositions and Missions (CITEM), which serves as the department's export promotions arm, and the Export Marketing Bureau (EMB), which oversees the development, promotion, and monitoring of Philippine exports (M. Solina, personal communication, September 22, 2023), contribute to promoting Philippine exports (Department of Trade and Industry, n.d.). Apart from the mentioned stakeholders, Local Government Units (LGUs) are also supplementary actors operating within the intersecting spheres of culture and tourism, promoting local cuisine by leveraging food festivals, diverse gastronomic events, and cultural exchange programs.

International Cultural Associations play a crucial role in gastrodiplomacy by utilizing food festivals, food receptions, food demonstrations, and showcases as their instruments within the spheres of tourism and culture. A noteworthy illustration of this dynamic is the Filipino Community Organizing Committee (FCOC) playing a crucial role in uniting the Filipino community in their host countries (Embassy of the Philippines Bangkok, 2015) . Further enhancing this global connection are various associations, such as the Association of Filipinos in Thailand (AFT), the Philippine-Thai Business Club (PTBC), and the United Filipinos in Thailand (UFT). Beyond these community-driven efforts, entities such as the *Foro de Debate S.L.,* a gastronomy event organization based in Madrid, Spain, indirectly practice gastrodiplomacy by organizing fairs, congresses, and promotional events (Embassy of the Philippines Madrid, 2015). Similarly, the *Arum Estrategias Internacionalización* supports gastrodiplomacy by assisting Filipino food businesses in expanding their presence in international markets, contributing to cultural diplomacy and economic growth (Tiu, 2014). Meanwhile, the Philippine Cultural Association Braunschweig diligently promotes Filipino culture and cuisine in Germany. Through a series of cultural events and initiatives, this association significantly enhances cultural exchange and contributes to the broader goals of gastrodiplomacy (Embassy of the Philippines, Berlin, 2015). On another front, the Filipino Community Council of the ACT (FILCCA) operates as a unifying entity for Filipino Australians and Filipinos residing in Australia, contributing to cultural diplomacy efforts. Established in 1990, FILCCA serves as an essential connection, empowering and uplifting the Filipino community in Australia (Department of Foreign Affairs, Republic of the Philippines, 2015). While not explicitly centered on gastrodiplomacy, the Asia Society also plays a significant role as a non-profit organization dedicated to promoting mutual understanding and strengthening partnerships among Asian countries and the United States (Asia Society, 2019). Through facilitating dialogues, cultural exchanges, and collaborations, the Asia Society indirectly contributes to the global promotion of Philippine culture and cuisine.

Public culinary personalities and restaurateurs within the intersecting spheres of culture, business, and tourism employ food receptions, festivals and fairs, culinary tours, and pop-up restaurants. In particular, Philippine restaurateurs and Filipino chefs, including renowned figures such as Pepe Dayaw, Amy Besa and Chef Romy Dorotan of Purple Yam Restaurant, and Chef Margarita Forés, play pivotal roles in propelling Philippine gastrodiplomacy to new heights. For instance, Pepe Dayaw's *Nowhere Kitchen* integrates various artistic elements, blending performance art, design concepts, and narrative cooking – emphasizing resourceful creativity, much like crafting art from leftovers (Embassy of the Philippines, 2020). Also, Chef Margarita Forés was instrumental in persuading the former Secretary of Tourism at the Philippines Department of Tourism regarding the significant benefits of hosting an international event, *Madrid Fusion Manila*, to bolster tourism through gastronomy (Interface Tourism Spain, 2017). Moreover, inspired by the diverse experiences of migrant communities, Amy Besa and her husband, Chef Romy Dorotan were both recognized well before the emergence of popular spots like *Maharlika or Jeepney* in New York or the *Filipino Food Movement* (Yadao, 2015). Beyond their culinary ventures, their focus on preservation and a return to traditional cooking techniques is evident, reflected in Amy's establishment of the *Ang Sariling Atin (Food That Was Always Ours) Culinary Heritage Institute* in the Philippines (Yadao, 2015; Heritage Radio Network, n.d).

Businesses and corporations operate within the spheres of both business and culture, strategically employing trade shows and culinary festivals as instruments. A compelling example comes from Jollibee Inc., a rapidly expanding restaurant company with international operations (Department of Foreign Affairs, 2018). Though its primary focus is not gastrodiplomacy, Jollibee is pivotal in introducing Filipino flavors to global palates through its international branches, thereby significantly contributing to cultural exchange. Similarly, Yellow Cab Pizza Co., a pizza restaurant chain originating in the Philippines, is expanding its presence to countries like Cambodia, where it introduces innovative, Filipino-inspired pizza flavors (Philippine Embassy in Cambodia, 2020). Meanwhile, Seafood City, the most prominent Filipino/Asian supermarket chain in the US and Canada, is crucial in promoting Filipino food products and ingredients within the diaspora by serving as a bridge to Filipino cuisine (Department of Foreign Affairs, n.d.). Akin to this, Lulu Hypermarket, a prominent retail chain in the Middle East, collaborates with the Philippine Embassy in Riyadh and Qatar to champion Filipino food products (Philippine Embassy, Riyadh, 2015). Events like *Pinoy Fiesta* hosted by Lulu prominently showcased Filipino cuisine and products, effectively nurturing cultural and economic diplomacy. In addition, Fisher Farms, Inc. (FFI) stands as the Philippines' primary provider of farm-raised seafood, catering to diverse markets by offering a wide array of premium, fresh frozen, and value-added seafood products both domestically and internationally (Cahiles-Magkilat, 2022). Furthermore, Ayala Malls, in collaboration with the Department of Tourism, hosts the *Kain Na! food and travel festival,* serving as an effective platform for promoting Filipino culinary delights (Department of Tourism, 2022). Lastly, the Philippine-American Chamber of Commerce - Pennsylvania (PACC-PA) also plays a vital role in promoting Filipino cuisine in the United States. Its event, *Taste of the Philippines,* held at the iconic Reading Terminal Market, showcases the best of Filipino cuisine (Consulate General of the Republic of the Philippines New York, 2018).

The primary and supplementary agents driving Philippine gastrodiplomacy include state actors like the Department of Tourism (DOT), the National Commission for Culture and the Arts (NCCA), and the Department of Foreign Affairs (DFA), as well as non-state entities such as the Filipino Food Movement, Mama Sita's, and Kulinarya Qatar. Alongside governmental agencies, international cultural associations, public culinary figures, and businesses, these agents utilize various platforms and initiatives to promote Filipino cuisine globally. Through festivals, bazaars, food-month celebrations, expos, and online campaigns, they showcase the nation's culinary heritage, enhancing its cultural identity on the world stage. By leveraging their networks and resources, these actors amplify the essence of Filipino cuisine, garnering global interest and appreciation and ultimately shaping the trajectory of Philippine gastrodiplomacy.

Actors' Generated Influence and Attraction

Philippine gastrodiplomacy has influenced target audiences to cultivate a favorable disposition towards the Philippines through two approaches. The first approach involves the Philippines' expansion of its network resources to establish and enhance the nation's brand through its culinary heritage. This expansion is characterized by both exclusive collaboration, where agents of the exact nature combine their resources to attract targeted audiences, and inclusive collaboration, where agents expand partnerships to agents of a different nature. The second approach encompasses selective sustainability, which combines limited long-term initiatives and high-yield one-time events.

Raimzhanova's (2015) *scale* refers to the extent of human resources and non-human resources involved in the execution of soft power initiatives. In Philippine gastrodiplomacy, state and non-state actors have expanded their human and non-human resources by strategically employing exclusive collaboration. Exclusive collaboration generates influence and attraction by fostering a concentrated and coordinated approach between entities of a similar nature and shared characteristics, such as state actors collaborating among themselves or non-state actors working together. This approach involves the strategic pooling of resources, expertise, and capabilities (White et al., 2019). While actors in gastrodiplomacy have opted for this strategy for convenience and efficiency, it risks limiting diversity in perspectives and approaches. Nevertheless, expanding network resources has played a pivotal role in strengthening the collaborative effort and the ability to attract diverse audiences.

First Secretary Monastrial of the Philippine Embassy in Madrid highlighted the improved budget and execution of planned activities enabled through their collaboration with the Department of Tourism (personal communication, October 5, 2023).

State actors have demonstrated exclusive collaboration through events like the *International Food Exhibition Philippines (IFEX)*, which was a major international trade show illustrating the partnership between the Department of Trade and Industry's Center for International Trade Expositions and Missions (DTI-CITEM) and the Department of Agriculture (DA) and the Bureau of Fisheries and Aquatic Resources (BFAR). The event provided a venue for local businesses to connect with international buyers, distributors, and industry professionals, fostering trade partnerships and opening up opportunities for market expansion (Business Mirror, 2018). Another example is the collaboration between the Department of Tourism (DOT), the Department of Agriculture (DA), and the Department of Trade and Industry's Farm Tourism Program (DTI). They collaborated to pool their resources to implement new initiatives to promote the agricultural sector, enhancing the appeal of their location and produce (Rocamora, 2017). Meanwhile, non-state actors have also exhibited exclusive collaboration. For instance, Mama Sita has partnered with Chef Claude Tayag to promote Adobo with the launch of his book, Adobo Books, thereby championing Filipino culinary tradition and expanding their influence (Nepomuceno-Gamad, personal communication, September 23, 2023). Additionally, the Filipino Food Movement Australia has actively engaged with local chefs, cookbook authors, restaurant owners, food bloggers, and expert home cooks through their events, like *Sahog,* an initiative encouraging partnership within the Fili-Aus community (Edo, 2020). These examples of exclusive collaboration demonstrate efficient working relationships. Still, its limited scope to similar entities may hinder the desired global influence, compelling agents to expand their resources through inclusive collaboration.

Inclusive collaboration broadens the agent's human and

non-human resources by engaging diverse actors beyond those of a similar nature (White et al., 2019). The data highlighted inclusive collaboration among state and non-state actors in organizing *the Philippines' Filipino Food Month 2022*, led by the Department of Agriculture (DA), the Department of Tourism (DOT), the National Commission for Culture and the Arts (NCCA), and the Philippine Culinary Heritage Movement (PCHM). Clang Garcia also emphasized the role of collaborating with diverse actors to elevate Filipino culinary initiatives to a national and global level (personal communication, September 14, 2023). Additionally, from 2015 to 2017, the Department of Tourism (DOT) led the Philippines' participation in *Madrid Fusion Spain*, collaborating with the Philippine Embassy in Madrid, the Department of Agriculture (DA), and Filipino chefs to showcase Filipino cuisine and culture globally. Concurrently, *Madrid Fusion Manila* events, organized by the Philippine Department of Tourism (DOT), the Tourism Promotions Board (TPB), Spanish organizations *Forode Debate* and *Arum Estrategias Internacionalizacion*, along with the Department of Agriculture (DA) and Department of Trade and Industry (DTI), celebrated the historical ties between the two nations and aimed to establish the Philippines as a gastronomic hub. These examples of inclusive collaboration demonstrate the efforts of agents to create more effective and sustainable initiatives that generate substantial and long-lasting impacts on target audiences.

Raimzhanova (2015) also highlights the role of *sustainability* in generating long-lasting and enduring influence of initiatives to maintain the legitimacy of the agent's use of its instruments. The data showed that Philippine gastrodiplomacy actors had generated influence through limited long-term initiatives and high-yield one-time initiatives. While state actors' structured long-term initiatives offer stability, they are constrained by inflexibility and susceptibility to shifts in state priorities. In contrast, non-state actors' initiatives are more flexible but limited by resource constraints, leading them to prioritize high-yield one-time initiatives.

State actors' approach to pre-planning is guided by their compliance with the Government Procurement Reform Act (Republic Act No. 9184, 2002), which mandates them to submit an Annual Procurement Plan (APP) outlining the timeline and budget for their initiatives prepared one year in advance. For example, First Secretary Monastrial (personal communication, October 5, 2023) emphasized the significant role of *Philippine Independence Day* as a key gastrodiplomacy initiative in Spain that has been consistently pursued annually from 2015-2022. However, she highlighted the challenge of distributing the remaining funds to finance events initially excluded from the APP. This challenge shows how the state actors' pre-planned approach imposes constraints on the flexibility of the number of initiatives they can undertake through-out the year. Additionally, long-term initiatives are based on the prevailing administration's interest. Planning Officer Canceran from the Department of Agriculture (DA) highlighted that the consistency of gastrodiplomacy initiatives changes over time based on the current administration's priority. An example is the state actors' fluctuating support for Chef Jam Melchor's Philippine culinary initiatives, which initially thrived during Chairman Felipe de Leon Jr.'s tenure in the National Commission for Culture and the Arts (NCCA). However, Chef Melchor encountered challenges following De Leon's departure, prompting Chef Melchor to resort to an online petition that called on former President Rodrigo Roa Duterte to declare April as *Filipino Food Month* (Melchor, 2016). This petition, championed by Former Agriculture Secretary Emmanuel Piñol, led to the signing of Presidential Decree 469 in 2018, which established *Filipino Food Month*.

In the case of non-state actors, long-term initiatives are similarly characterized by their pre-planned nature, rooted in their interests and the track record of successes at the event. For example, Kulinarya Qatar has organized its *Filipino Food Festival* annually based on member suggestions and majority agreement (personal communication, October 10, 2023), while the Mama Sita Foundation has selected initiatives like the *International Food Exhibition (IFEX)* based on past success and alignment with their mission of global food accessibility (personal communication, September 23, 2023). Despite its flexibility, the limited number of long-term initiatives undertaken by non-state actors compared to state actors can be attributed to financial constraints. Ms. Anna Manlulo, the president of Filipino Food Movement Australia (FFMA) (personal communication, October 13, 2023), expressed the organization's hopes to make their projects sustainable but is faced with the challenge of limited resources. She conveyed that their current long-term initiatives, such as the *Mabuhay Nights* and *Meryenda* gathering, are hindered by a lack of funding and volunteers, as they are financing them independently. The data revealed the link between the *sustainability* of an initiative and the *scale* of human and non-human resources, diminishing the effectiveness of non-state actors' conduct of gastrodiplomacy and compelling them to resort to high-yield one-time events.

The state and non-state actors' conduct of gastrodiplomacy is also characterized by high-yield one-time initiatives. Despite the state actors' structured approach, there are instances where state actors recognized the importance of unplanned opportunities (Philippine Embassy in Doha, Qatar, personal communication, October 9, 2023). While these one-time initiatives may be embraced when their benefits are apparent, efforts are made to minimize their costs. A unique opportunity that incurred minimal costs was the attendance of the Philippine Consulate General in Auckland at the *Hapunan* event organized by students from the Auckland University of Technology (Embassy of the Philippines Welling-ton, New Zealand, 2015). The Philippine Consulate General in Auckland recognized the event as beneficial, as it perceived that it "contributes to deeper understanding and goodwill between the Philippines and New Zealand." However, while these events offer unique opportunities for state actors, they may be hindered by their lack of follow-up activities or integration into a broader, long-term gastrodiplomacy initiative.

In the context of non-state actors, one-time initiatives are often conducted due to budget constraints, aiming to maximize their initiative's impact within their financial constraints. An example is the 2017 *Hidden Flavors of the Philippines Kitchen Culinary Tour* organized by Amy Besa, the founder of Purple Yam (Department of Foreign Affairs, 2017). Despite the tour's one-time nature, the scope of such an initiative, spanning across different locations, indicated the actor's interest in maximizing the impact of their initiative. Furthermore, the strategic alignment of one of its tours in Philadelphia with Filipino-American History Month showcased a deliberate effort to capitalize on the celebration and draw a bigger audience. Another example is Pepe Dayaw's participation in the *Berlin Food Art Week* through his performance entitled *"Dayaw: Cooking Filipino Contemporary"*(Embassy of the Philippines, Berlin, 2015). His performance showcased his culinary talents and featured a pop-up restaurant for the German public. However, his initiative did not see recurrence and was limited to a specific location, constraining the impact of his activity within the area and within that period.

In essence, the actors of Philippine gastrodiplomacy strategically generate influence and attraction through the expansion of network sources and selective sustainability. The expansion of network resources is characterized by exclusive collaboration, where state and non-state actors focus on similar entities to enhance impact, and inclusive collaboration, which broadens partnerships beyond similar entities. Meanwhile, selective sustainability involves a dual strategy of limited long-term initiatives and high-yield one-time initiatives. Thus, the Philippines strategically balances collaboration strategies and sustainability measures to wield a nuanced and impactful presence in global gastrodiplomacy. This not only showcases the country's culinary richness but also positions it as a strategic player in international relations.

New Mindsets and Views about the Philippines

The data gathered showed that Philippine gastrodiplomacy's agents have generated influence and attraction by expanding network resources and implementing selective sustainability measures.

Consequently, the influence generated by the actors has led to the forming of two prominent views about the country among their target audiences. The first is the view of the Philippines as an emerging culinary destination with diverse yet untapped culinary resources, shaped by the country's increasing culinary appeal to foreign audiences and the diversification of its trade. The second is the view of Philippine cuisine as a newly enabled source of diasporic identity and profession, drawn from Overseas Filipino Workers (OFWs) and Filipino Restaurateurs abroad. The exercise of Philippine soft power has instilled these views into its international audiences: foreigners and diaspora alike.

The first view of the Philippines as an emerging culinary destination with diverse culinary resources is centered on two premises. The first premise is that the Philippines further embodied an internationally expansive, evolving, and attractive culinary experience. On the international stage, Philippine Gastrodiplomacy's agents conduct a public promotions campaign through events like the *2019 Melbourne Food and Wine Festival* or the *DC Pinoy Festival.* These events, attended by both public audiences and celebrity chefs like Anthony Bourdain, have received positive receptions, with Bourdain noting it as delicious and "underrated" (Romualdez, 2019; Philippine Embassy of Canberra Australia, 2019). Further state and non-state efforts internationally, such as Filipino cuisine's inclusion on Instagram's 10 World's Most Popular Cuisine; acclamation of owners and chefs like Washington DC's Bad Saint, whose Chef Tom Cunanan was awarded the Best Chef Mid-Atlantic Category 2019; Los Angeles' Ma'am Sir under Chef Charles Olaila earning a spot on "Best Restaurants in America for 2019", show that interest and appreciation in Philippine cuisine grew because of these breakthroughs (De Guzman Quadra, 2021).

In tandem with outside efforts would be efforts inside the Philippines to build up that image of a culinary melting pot, the first significant effort being the *Madrid Fusion Manila,* which ran from 2016-2018. According to Ms. Fay Lena Castro from the Department of Tourism (personal communication, 2023),

Madrid Fusion Manila's significance transcended borders by bringing together top culinary experts in Manila, underscoring Asia's rising culinary prominence. Within *Madrid Fusion Manila*, several smaller, interconnected events like the *World Street Food Congress* and the *World Street Dialogue* featured international and Filipino speakers from the culinary world. The participation of influential figures significantly enhanced the global perception of Philippine cuisine (Adel, 2017). Moreover, foreign initiatives to explore Philippine cuisine are evident outside these events. For instance, Anna Olson discussed her Filipino collaborations with culinary stars Margarita Forés, Claude Tayag, and Rob Pengson on her show "Inspired by Anna Olson," expressing her positive experiences, insights into regional cooking styles, and admiration for both traditional and innovative practices (Tayag, 2016). Olson appreciated the honesty she found in Filipino cuisine, describing it as fulfilling and reminiscent of comforting home-cooked meals.

It is not just celebrity chefs who are interested in Filipino cuisine and actively promoting it. Many public audience members, including home chefs, bloggers, and others, are also interested. For example, Selena Gomez prepared adobo and turon with the assistance of Fil-Am chef Jordan Andino on her HBO show Selena + Chef (Philstar Life, 2021). Additionally, the Philippine Embassy in Doha, Qatar (personal communication, 2023) mentioned that a Canadian food influencer approached the embassy to collaborate with them for the *Filipino Food Month*, illustrating the growing role of influences in gastrodiplomacy. This sentiment was echoed by First Secretary and Consul Carlyn Monastrial of the Philippine embassy in Madrid (personal communication, 2023), who emphasized the importance of online influencers in reaching the younger demographic. Similarly, the Philippine mission in South Korea, led by H.E. Maria Theresa B. Dizon-De Vega (personal communication, 2023), has focused on engaging with diverse actors, including influencers, to attract their target audience. Looking at influencers from a different perspective, they don't always need to be tapped after forming a positive image; they can take the initiative to promote gastrodiplomacy. Mark Wiens, a traveler and food blogger, traveled to different countries, including the Philippines, to learn about their culture and food (Lariosa, 2022).

However, achieving this positive perception of the Philippines has been challenging, as for every dish that gains acclaim in a Taste Atlas, others have gained global notoriety (De Guzman Quadra, 2021). Filipino cuisine's appeal often depends on meeting international standards, including presentation, food safety, and health considerations. Traditional Filipino dishes may be hit or miss for foreign audiences, and recent advances in gastrodiplomacy have leveraged aspects of Filipino cuisine that align with global tastes. Canadian-born Filipino chef Rechie Valdez has emphasized the importance of appealing presentation and taste (Palma, n.d.). Therefore, adjustments to traditional recipes are crucial for advancing Philippine gastrodiplomacy. However, current efforts in this regard are limited and would benefit from institutionalization and a structured approach to mainstream Filipino cuisine. Philippine gastrodiplomacy aims to attract foreign audiences who will benefit the country materially by fostering a positive perception. However, this goal may not be fully realized as state and non-state actors operate independently without a centralized institution or structure to disseminate knowledge and resources. This lack of coordination may hinder the potential success of Philippine gastrodiplomacy compared to its more prosperous neighbors.

Additionally, the view of the Philippines as an emerging culinary destination builds upon its pre-existing image as a trading partner, which has transformed through the diversification and innovation of the Filipino food trade. Before 2015, there was already a demand for Filipino food, but the country's food exports accounted for only 3.02 percent of its total trade export value (Observer of Economic Complexity, 2016). However, from 2015 to 2022, Filipino cuisine gained international attention and praise, making this export percentage more significant (Good News Filipinas Team, 2017; Logarta, 2018). With increased recognition of the Philippines' culinary resources, the country expanded its range of food products for export and complied with global food safety standards. For instance, in 2016, the Philippines became the top tuna exporter to the European Union, valued at USD 12 million (Good News Filipinas Team, 2017). China also contacted the Philippines, collaborating with the Department of Trade and Industry (DTI) to attract Filipino enterprises to participate in the Chinese International Import Expo (CIIE) (Bo, 2018). This collaboration led to vital trade deals in health, organic, and premium food products, increasing sales each year (Crismundo, 2021; Department of Trade and Industry, 2022).

Despite the challenges posed by the COVID-19 pandemic, there were incremental advances in foreign markets in Singapore and Australia in 2021-2022. In Singapore, locally available Filipino ingredients were showcased in curated dishes at the *World Food Summit* (Vicencio-Luz, 2022). In Australia, Philippine food offerings expanded to 200 Woolworth stores, with plans for further expansion (Embassy of the Philippines, Canberra, 2021). Noteworthy advancements included the first shipment of uncooked shrimp to Australia in 2022, facilitated by collaborative efforts between businesses and agencies from both countries (Department of Trade and Industry, 2022). In South Korea, public interest in Philippine agri-food products was evident, with over sixty thousand people visiting the Philippine pavilion during the *2021 International Agricultural Exhibition*, while negotiations for the Philippines-Republic of Korea Free Trade Agreement recently concluded (Unite, 2021). These developments highlight a growing surge of interest in Philippine agri-food products.

If the initial phase of Philippine gastrodiplomacy aimed to promote Filipino food to create a positive image widely, the next logical step is to ensure common accessibility to these products, facilitating true global mainstreaming. However, for this to happen, the state and its agencies must recognize their role in creating the conditions for globalization. This endeavor has inherent risks, including the dilemma of whether to prioritize high-profit food products for export or continue developing diverse regional offerings. The Philippines faces the paradox of being both a food exporter and an importer, with a population experiencing food insecurity (Dunaway & Macabuac, 2022). Pursuing high-profit exports reinforces stereotypes and allows foreign markets to dictate what constitutes Filipino food while developing regional cuisine, which requires significant time and resources. The Philippines must choose a course of action and mitigate the consequences accordingly. Currently, the uncoordinated actions of various agents result in conflicting approaches, as the Philippines simultaneously pursues both strategies. This can undermine the country's reputation as a food trading hub if it struggles to meet domestic food demands while commodifying its cuisine or fails to showcase its full range of regional styles due to resource constraints. These conflicting efforts, coupled with entrenched conceptions and a lack of abundant food supplies, stem from the absence of a systemic approach to Philippine gastrodiplomacy. Without such an approach, the environment for introducing new food products or changing negative perceptions remains unfavorable, limiting the potential benefits (Dunaway & Macabuac, 2022).

The second view of the Philippine cuisine as a renewed source of diasporic identity and profession is drawn from Overseas Filipino Workers (OFWs) and Filipino restaurateurs abroad who are also part of Philippine Gastrodiplomacy's target audience. To the OFWs, Filipino cuisine has become something worth promoting and supporting to express solidarity and identity. The Filipino diaspora, often described as resilient and adaptable *"bagong bayani,"* presents a paradox when considering their active involvement in gastrodiplomacy alongside their assimilation into host societies (Roces, 2021). Grassroots efforts to promote Filipino cuisine globally were initially modest and unsuccessful, partly due to cultural factors such as the Filipino tendency toward "hiya" or shame (Zubiri, 2021). Moreover, the early diaspora lacked culinary expertise, hindering culinary outreach abroad (Business World, 2020; Ramar Foods, 2015). However, with the diaspora's increasing numbers, efforts emerged to meet the unmet demand for Filipino products. In the US, the Ramar Foods Group's *Kusina* initiative introduced Filipino food products in 2012, laying the groundwork for a growing market presence (Ramar Foods, 2015). As subsequent generations rediscovered their Filipino heritage, promoting culinary traditions became a means of expressing identity (McNeilly, 2017). The diaspora's embrace of Filipino cuisine reflected national pride and signaled receptiveness among foreign audiences to promote Filipino food (McNeilly, 2017; Philippine Embassy in Qatar, personal communication, 2023). As Clang Garcia noted in an interview, the diaspora serves as a primary market for Filipino cuisine, with Filipinos abroad preserving and sharing their cultural palate (personal communication, 2023).

The Filipino diaspora plays a crucial role in facilitating the entry of Filipino food products into foreign markets, serving as natural ambassadors for spreading Filipino cuisine. However, due to limited supply, only a few select foods are promoted as "national," while regional offerings remain scarce. Efforts to expand into new markets, such as the US, have ventured beyond traditional staples to include fine dining and fusion cuisine, catering to diverse tastes (Fulton, 2016). The sizable Filipino community abroad has supported such initiatives, helping to mitigate the impact of failed endeavors. While individual agents have made strides independently, institutionalizing and systematizing support can maximize benefits and expand networks. Moreover, efforts to promote Filipino cuisine have attracted diaspora members back to their roots, contributing to preserving regional cooking styles and combating brain drain. Personalities like Raphael Teraoka Dacones and Bruce Ricketts have returned to the Philippines, drawn by renewed optimism and pride (Mok, 2017). Initiatives such as the Department of Tourism's *Chefs' Food Trip* have invited Filipino-American chefs to engage with local culinary traditions, fostering cultural exchange and connection (Jay, 2020). Ultimately, embracing Filipino cuisine represents a multifaceted statement of association with the Philippines, reflecting political, cultural, and economic ties.

To chefs and restaurant owners, the focus is less on pride and more on what it means for their livelihood through business growth and career advancement. Before 2015, chefs and restaurateurs from the Filipino diaspora had limited visibility and involvement in Philippine gastrodiplomacy due to assimilation concerns and supply challenges. International chefs hesitated to feature Filipino cuisine on their menus, fearing loss of customers (Golangco, 2021). However, this began to change as the availability of Filipino food products increased, leading to recognition for innovators like Chef Margarita Forés, who was named Asia's Best Female Chef in 2016 (Good News Filipinas Team, 2017). Chef Forés noted a growing national pride in Filipino cuisine, signaling a shift in attitudes among the diaspora (Good News Filipinas Team, 2017). This newfound environment allowed for the open promotion of Filipino cuisine. With this shift, opportunities emerged for chefs to specialize in Filipino cuisine as a viable career path, supported by a growing global market. Establishments like Abaca in San Francisco, recognized by Esquire as one of America's Best New Restaurants in 2021, and Chef Cathal's Kaliwa, endorsed by Anthony Bourdain, exemplify the success of Filipino culinary ventures (Grana, 2022; Tagala, 2018). Chef Cathal noted that the absence of preconceived notions about Filipino cuisine contributed to its appeal, highlighting the need for chefs to manage audience expectations (Tagala, 2018). Moving forward, maintaining authenticity while managing hype will be essential for Philippine gastrodiplomacy agents.

However, achieving this necessitates managing diverse views among restaurateurs on the best approach to introducing Filipino cuisine, with two diverging opinions. The first approach focuses on enhancing mainstream global dishes with Filipino influences, proposing to pair techniques from the homeland with foreign cuisine to serve as a gateway for introducing audiences to Filipino flavors (Fulton, 2016; Inquirer.net US Bureau, 2016). The second approach advocates for exposing global audiences to traditional Filipino cuisine by sourcing ingredients locally, aiming to acclimate them to the culture, tastes, and regional dishes (Logarta, 2018).

This approach fosters a direct patron relationship between buyers and farmers, profiting both in the long term and benefiting the Philippines (Clang Garcia, personal communication, 2023). However, this approach faces challenges due to the diverse nature of Filipino cuisine, reflecting the country's multiethnicity, resulting in a lack of cohesion or consensus on what constitutes Filipino cuisine (Business World, 2020; Ige Ramos, personal communication, 2023). This fragmented conception is likely carried by the diaspora, leading to the existence of two approaches—gradual versus immediate—and why the latter is easier to achieve, given the prevalence of certain dishes across the Philippines. Despite these divergent views, both are centered on Philippine cuisine as a new professional opportunity worth promoting abroad. The increased visibility and presence of chefs and restaurateurs in conducting gastrodiplomacy can be attributed to this mindset being instilled in them. There is also a trend towards collaborations in various initiatives and the creation of support networks. However, what would be most beneficial for restaurant growth is a global program similar to Global Thai, where institutionalized Philippine Gastrodiplomacy could assist upcoming enterprises while being subject to a review and accreditation process. Furthermore, expanding and centralizing the global supply of Filipino ingredients is crucial to effectively meet the growing foreign demand and support mainstreaming Filipino cuisine.

Two predominant views of the Philippines have emerged from foreign and Filipino diaspora target audiences. The first portrays the Philippines as an emerging culinary destination rich in diverse yet underutilized culinary resources. The second view presents Philippine cuisine as a potent source of diasporic identity and professional opportunity. These perspectives hold significance for different audiences of Philippine gastrodiplomacy. The former is particularly important for international audiences, signaling the Philippines' potential as a trade partner for new food products in demand and as a culinary tourist hotspot. State agencies must, therefore, create conditions conducive to facilitating trade and access to food products while ensuring a steady supply to meet growing international demand. The latter view holds significance for the Filipino diaspora, serving as a source of identity and pride as Philippine cuisine gains acclaim and positive attention. This has led to increased support for Filipino establishments abroad and a greater willingness to purchase and consume Filipino food. For chefs and restaurateurs, this view has made Filipino cuisine and restaurants a viable livelihood and career path outside the Philippines, turning them into unofficial culinary ambassadors and culinary outposts for Philippine gastrodiplomacy. Ultimately, the target audience for Philippine gastrodiplomacy, comprising both international audiences and the diaspora, demonstrates a positive disposition towards the Philippines, prompting them to act in ways that benefit the nation, whether consciously or otherwise.

Conclusions and Recommendations

The Philippines actively pursues gastrodiplomacy, yet its efforts lack cohesion and sustainability, prompting the need to comprehend its underlying components for optimal outcomes. This research delineated two categories of Philippine gastrodiplomacy agents: *primary agents*, who primarily promote Filipino cuisine to foster positive international relations, and *supplementary agents*, encompassing entities promoting Filipino food without a primary focus on international relations. Furthermore, these agents employed two strategic methods: the *expansion of network resources* and *selective sustainability*. As a result of these methods, emerging mindsets about the Philippines recognized the country as a *culinary destination* and positioned *Filipino cuisine as a pivotal source of diasporic identity*. Based on these findings, the research concludes that Philippine gastrodiplomacy is incomplete due to its lack of full institutionalization into a unified system and clear objectives, resulting in inconsistent efforts beyond the diaspora. In order to address these shortcomings, future research should include the recipients of Philippine gastrodiplomacy for a more comprehensive understanding. Additionally, policy recommendations advocate for the institutionalization of Philippine gastrodiplomacy to support Filipino restaurants and startups while integrating the diaspora into this structured framework. In implementing these measures, Philippine Gastrodiplomacy can transition from a strategy to an institutionalized and unified system. This transition ensures the full realization of its potential, maximizing its positive impact on international relations and enhancing the nation's international image.

Acknowledgements

We express our deepest gratitude to our thesis mentor, Ms. Monica Villa Abrille, MAS, for her constant supervision and generous insights that guided us throughout this study. We also express our gratitude to our thesis adviser, Mr. John Harvey Gamas, MA, for his invaluable support. Our sincere appreciation is extended to our esteemed panelists, Ms. Krizza Janica Mahinay, MA, Ms. Rhisan Mae Morales, MA, and Ms. Rhodalie Emilio, MPA, for sharing their expertise and constructive criticism.

References

Adel, R. (2017, May 11). *Anthony Bourdain, Filipino chefs to speak at World Street Food Congress 2017 Dialogue.* Philstar.com; Philstar.com. https://www.philstar.com/ lifestyle/food-and-leisure/2017/05/11/1698952/anthony-bourdain-filipino-chefs-speak-world-street-food-congress-2017-dialogue

Asia Society (2019). About Asia Society. Retrieved November 15, 2023 from https://asiaso ciety.org/about

Asiddao, A. (n.d.). *PH Brings A "Festival Of Flavors" To CH Import Expo.* Retrieved on: November 21, 2023 from: https://foodphilippines.com/ story/ph-brings-a-festival-of-flavors-to-ch-import-expo/

Bo, X. (February, 2018). *China to hold roadshows to invite Philippine business to participa te in first int'l import expo: embassy.* Retrieved on: October 28, 2023 from: https://w ww.xinhuanet.com/english/2018-02-28/c_137006391.html

Business Mirror. (2018, March 6). Ifex Philippines 2018 makes waves with exciting seafood edition BusinessMirror. https://businessmirror.com.ph/2018/03/06/ifex-philippines-2018-makes-waves-with-exciting-sea-food-edition/

Business World, (August, 2020). Why Pinoy food is not as famous as other Asian cuisines. Retrieved on: November 13, 2023 from: https://www.bworldonline.com/editors-picks/2020/08/06/309434/why-pinoy-food-is-not-as-famous-as-other-asian-cuisin es/

Cahiles-Magkilat. (2022). *PH now exports uncooked shrimps to Australia.* Manila

Bulletin. https://mb.com.ph/2022/06/10/ph-now-exports-uncooked-shrimps-to-australia

Creswell, J. W. (2013). *Qualitative Inquiry and Research Design: Choosing Among Five Approaches* (3rd ed.). SAGE Publications.

Crismundo, K. (2021, July 12). *Standards for Pinoy cuisine meant for int'l promotion: DTI*. Philippine News Agency. Retrieved March 12, 2023, from https://www.pna.gov.ph /articles/1146747

Cruz, B. (2022, October 31). Filipino American History Month a Period of Commemoration Reflection and Diplomatic Action. https://moor-parkreporter.com/4018351/showcase/filipino-american-history-month-a-pe-riod-of-commemoration-reflection-and-diplomatic-action/

Daza-Puyat N. (October, 2019). *La Petite Manille mounts the first Filipino food festival in France.* Retrieved on: November 21, 2023 from: https://mb.com.ph/ 2019/10/26/la-petite-manille-mounts-the-first-filipino-food-festival-in-france/

De Guzman Quadra, M.H. (February, 2021). *Filipino food is Top 10 World's Most Popular Cuisine on Instagram.* Retrieved on: November 12, 2023 from: https://goodnewspilipinas.com/filipino-food-is-top-10-worlds-most-popular-cuisine-on-instagram/

Department of Foreign Affairs, Republic of the Philippines (2018, June 15) Philippine embassy celebrates "Kalayaan 2015" with Filipinos in Moscow. Facebook. https://shorturl.at/mqzR9

Department of Foreign Affairs. (2017, September 25). *Philippine embassy in Seoul actively promotes Phl products, cuisine and tourism.* Department of Foreign Affairs. Retrieved March 3, 2017, from https://dfa.gov.ph/dfa-news/news-from-our-foreign-service-postsupdate/14250-philippine-em-bassy-in-seoul-actively-promote s-phl-products-cuisine-and-tourism

Department of Foreign Affairs. (2018, July). *Ph embassy in Beijing shares Filipinos' love for food via "Flavours of the Philippines".* Department of Foreign Affairs. Retrieved March 7, 2023, from https://dfa.gov.ph/ dfa-news/news-from-our-foreign -service-postsupdate/17331-ph-em-bassy-in-beijing-shares-filipinos-love-for-food-via-flavours-of-the-philip-pines?fbclid=IwAR3XMdBFVoyicM9JlOuuwvGi84kE ByXGNe540 A1XSgjwQ1rXn3XlwoNobs0

Department of Foreign Affairs. (2018). Jollibee UK officially opens to the public on 20 October 2018. Facebook. Retrieved November 15, 2023, from https://fb.watch/ okJhySWRMc/

Department of Foreign Affairs. (2019, April 26). PH Promotes Culture, Food, Tourism at 2nd ASEAN Bazaar. Retrieved November 16, 2023,.

Department of Foreign Affairs. (2020, September 3). *PH Embassy, PH Ag-riculture Office in Seoul, Mama Sita Foundation Launch "Traditional,*

Contemporary PH Cuisine: Lutong Bahay Ni Mama Sita."https://dfa.gov. ph/dfa-news/news-from-our-foreign-service-postsupdate/27556-ph-embassy-ph-agriculture-office-in-seoul-mama-sita-foundation-launch-traditional-contemporary-ph-cuisine-lutong-bahay-ni-mama-sita

Department of Foreign Affairs. (n.d.). *Filipina in France cooks Ph cuisine at food festival in Paris.* Department of Foreign Affairs. Retrieved March 12, 2023, from https://df a.gov.ph/dfa-news/news-from-our-foreign-service-postsupdate/25178-filipina-coo ks-in-france-promote-ph-cuisine-at-food-festival-in-paris

Department of Foreign Affairs. (n.d.). *Filipino community in Thailand to hold barrio fiesta 2016 in celebration of the 118th anniversary of declaration of Philippine independence.* Department of Foreign Affairs. Retrieved March 7, 2023, from https://bangkokpe.dfa.gov.ph/embassy-headlines/601-filipino-community-in-thail and-to-hold-barrio-fiesta-2016-in-celebration-of-the-118th-anniversary-of-declara tion-of-philippine-independence

Department of Foreign Affairs. (n.d.). *Media, bloggers get special introduction to Filipino cuisine.* Department of Foreign Affairs. Retrieved March 12, 2023, from https://dfa.gov.ph/dfa-news/news-from-our-foreign-service-postsupdate/25587-media-bloggers-get-special-introduction-to-filipino-cuisine

Department of Foreign Affairs. (n.d.). *Ph ambassador's luncheon promotes Filipino cuisine in Canberra.* Department of Foreign Affairs. Retrieved March 12, 2023, from https://dfa.gov.ph/dfa-news/news-from-our-foreign-service-postsupdate/24970-ph-ambassador-s-luncheon-promotes-filipino-cuisine-in-canberra

Department of Foreign Affairs. (n.d.). *Ph ambassador to Italy promotes Filipino cuisine among ambassadors of the UN ESCAP Asia Pacific group.* Department of Foreign Affairs. Retrieved March 12, 2023, from https://dfa.gov.ph/dfa-news/ news-from-our-foreign-service-postsupdate/24908-ph-ambassador-to-italy-promotes-filipino-cuisine-among-ambassadors-of-the-un-escap-asia-pacific-group

Department of Foreign Affairs. (n.d.). *Ph Consulate General in Honolulu Celebrates Filipino Food Week.* Department of Foreign Affairs. Retrieved November 15, 2023, fromhttps://dfa.gov.ph/dfa-news/news-from-our-foreignservicepostsupdate/23345 -ph-consulate-general-in-honolulu-celebrates-filipino-food week?fbclid=IwAR2E_5Rm_al8cOBtMXM-VP1dFoBSWeCMEpKW-f2L_KXSzGzN-U8XUZ51_msc

Department of Foreign Affairs. (n.d.). *Ph embassy in Brunei highlights Ph trade, cuisine, products in BIMP-EAGA tertiary industry forum showcase 2019, world Hala culinary championship 2019.* Wikipedia. Retrieved March 12, 2023, from https://dfa.gov.ph/dfa-news/news-from-our-foreign-service-postsupdate/25580-ph-embas sy-in-brunei-highlights-ph-trade-cuisine-products-in-bimp-eaga-tertiary-industry-forum-showcase-2019-world-halal-culinary-championship-2019

Department of Foreign Affairs. (n.d.). *Philippine embassy in Bangkok joins in the opening ceremony of the ASEAN cultural expo 2016.* Department of Foreign Affairs. Retrieved March 7, 2023, from https://bangkokpe.dfa.gov.ph/embassy-headlines/5 93-philippine-embassy-in-bangkok-joins-in-the-opening-ceremony-of-the-asean-cultural-expo-2016

Department of Foreign Affairs. (n.d.). *Philippines-China relations: Beyond the territorial disputes.* Department of Foreign Affairs. Retrieved March 7, 2023, from https://fsi. gov.ph/philippines-china-relations-beyond-the-territoral-disputes/

Department of Foreign Affairs. (n.d.). *Ph to showcase history, cuisine, arts at the 2019 Frankfurt book fair.* Department of Foreign Affairs. Retrieved March 12, 2023, from https://dfa.gov.ph/dfa-news/news-from-our-foreign-service-postsupdate/247 24-ph-to-showcase-history-cuisine-arts-at-the-2019-frankfurt-book-fair

Department of Foreign Affairs. (n.d.). *Ph tourism, culture, cuisine, drinks featured in St. Petersburg reception.* Department of Foreign Affairs. Retrieved March 12, 2023, from https://dfa.gov.ph/dfa-news/news-from-our-foreign-service-postsupdate/25342-ph-tourism-culture-cuisine-drinks-featured-in-st-petersburg-reception

Department of Foreign Affairs. (n.d.). *Pinay chef in Argentina launches book on Filipino cuisine.* Department of Foreign Affairs. Retrieved March 12, 2023, from https://dfa. gov.ph/dfa-news/news-from-our-foreign-service-postsupdate/25619-pinay-chef-in-argentina-launches-book-on-filipino-cuisine

Department of Foreign Affairs. (n.d.). *The Philippines hosts the 3rd Madrid fusion Manila top culinary event draws world's top chefs and food enthusiasts.* Department of Foreign Affairs. Retrieved March 7, 2023, from https://bangkokpe.dfa.gov.ph/embassy-headlines/699-the-philippines-hosts-the-3rd-madrid-fusion-manila-top-culina ry-event-draws-world-s-top-chefs-and-food-enthusiasts

Department of Foreign Affairs (2016, September 7). Diplomats, Russian Officials Join Festivities at the PH Street Fair in Moscow. Retrieved March 7, 2023, from https://dfa.gov.ph/dfa-news/news-from-our-foreign-service-postsupdate/10309-diplomats-russian-officials-join-festivities-at-ph-street-fair-in-moscow

Department of Foreign Affairs (2017, September 25). Philippine Embassy in Seoul Actively Promotes PHL Products, Cuisine, and Tourism. Retrieved March 7, 2023, from https://dfa.gov.ph/dfa-news/news-from-our-foreign-service-posts update/14250-philippine-embassy-in-seoul-actively-promotes-phl-products-cuisine-and-tourism

Department of Foreign Affairs (2017, September 25). Philippine Embassy in Seoul Actively Promotes PHL Products, Cuisine, and Tourism. Retrieved March 7, 2023, from https://dfa.gov.ph/dfa-news/news-from-our-foreign-service-posts update/14250-philippine-embassy-in-seoul-actively-promotes-phl-products-cuisine-and-touri sm

Department of Foreign Affairs (2019, March 28). PH Street Food, Other Filipino Favorites Showcased in Paris' International Gastronomy Village. Retrieved March 7, 2023, from https://dfa.gov.ph/dfa-news/news-from-our-foreign-service-postsupdate/20917-ph-street-food-other-filipino-favorites-showcased-in-paris-international-gastronomy-village

Department of Foreign Affairs (2020, December 10). PH Embassy in Hanoi Joins Annual International Food Festival. Retrieved March 7, 2023, from https://dfa.gov.ph/dfa-news/news-from-our-foreign-service-postsupdate/28354-ph-embassy-in-hanoi-joins-annual-international-food-festival

Department of Foreign Affairs (2020, December 19). Philippine Embassy in Ankara Holds Cooking Demonstration of PH Cuisine Featuring Mama Sita Products March 9, 2023 from https://dfa.gov.ph/dfa-news/news-from-our-foreign-service-postsupdat e/28486-philippine-embassy-in-ankara-holds-cooking-demonstration-of-ph-cuisin e-featuring-mama-sita-products

Department of Foreign Affairs (2020, December 3). PH Embassy Seoul and Mama Sita Promote PH Cuisine with Korean Chef. Retrieved March 7, 2023, from https://dfa. gov.ph/dfa-news/news-from-our-foreign-service-postsupdate/28312-ph-embassy-seoul-and-mama-sita-promote-ph-cuisine-with-korean-chef

Department of Foreign Affairs (2020, February 24). Leading Berlin Culinary School Cooks PH Cuisine. Retrieved March 9, 2023, from https://dfa.gov.ph/dfa-news/news-from-our-foreign-service-postsupdate/26035-leading-berlin-culinary-school-cooks-ph-cuisine-2

Department of Foreign Affairs (2020, February 26). PH Embassy in Rome Promotes Filipino Food at 11th Festival della Diplomazia. Retrieved March 7, 2023, from https://dfa.gov.ph/dfa-news/news-from-our-foreign-service-postsupdate/28070-ph-embassy-in-rome-promotes-filipino-food-at-11th-festival-della-diplomazia

Department of Foreign Affairs (2020, March 12). PH Cuisine, Food Products Featured in Mesa Palatina. Retrieved March 9, 2023, from https://dfa.gov.ph/dfa-news/news -from-our-foreign-service-postsupdate/26279-ph-cuisine-food-products-featured-in-mesa-palatina

Department of Foreign Affairs (2020, March 20). PH Cuisine, Spain-based Filipino Restaurants Featured in El País. March 9, 2023, from https://dfa. gov.ph/ dfa-news/dfa-releasesupdate/27548-dfa-promotes-home-cooked-filipino-cuisine-throu gh-online-show-simply-sarap

Department of Foreign Affairs (2020, October 14). APH Consulate General in Los Angeles Kicks Off Fil-Am History Month with the Launch of #LALovEat: Pinoy Food Stories. Retrieved March 7, 2023, from https://dfa.gov.ph/dfa-news /news-from-our-foreign-service-postsupdate/27941-ph-consulate-general-in-los-angeles-kicks-off-fil-am-history-month-with-the-launch-of-laloveat-pinoy-food-stories

Department of Foreign Affairs (2020, September 03). PH Embassy, PH Agriculture Office in Seoul, Mama Sita Foundation Launch "Traditional, Contemporary PH Cuisine: Lutong Bahay Ni Mama Sita." March 9, 2023, from https://dfa.gov.ph/dfa-news/news-from-our-foreign-service-postsup-date/27556-ph-embassy-ph-agricultu re-office-in-seoul-mama-sita-founda-tion-launch-traditional-contemporary-ph-cuis ine-lutong-bahay-ni-mama-sita

Department of Foreign Affairs (2021, April 5). Halal Filipino Cuisine Takes Center Stage at Local Tourism Event in Brunei. Retrieved March 7, 2023, from https://dfa.gov.ph/dfa-news/news-from-our-foreign-service-post-supdate/28809-halal-filipino-cuisine-takes-center-stage-at-local-tourism-event-in-brunei

Department of Foreign Affairs (2021, August 9). Pinoy Entrepreneurship Thrives As New Spot for Filipino Food Opens in Vancouver Amidst Pandemic. Retrieved March 7, 2023, from https://dfa.gov.ph/dfa-news/news-from-our-foreign-service-postsupdate/29350-pinoy-entrepreneurship-thrives-as-new-spot-for-filipino-food-opens-in-vancouver-amidst-pandemic

Department of Foreign Affairs (2021, December 1). PH Embassy Organizes First Kain Tayo Lets Eat Cuisine Workshop in Cairo. Retrieved March 7, 2023, from https://dfa.gov.ph/dfa-news/news-from-our-foreign-service-postsupdate/29805-ph-embassy-organizes-first-kain-tayo-let-s-eat-cuisine-workshop-in-cairo

Department of Foreign Affairs (2021, December 22). PH Embassy Partner with First Russian Female Michelin Chef to Promote Filipino Cuisine Tourism. Retrieved March 7, 2023, from: https://dfa.gov.ph/dfa-news/news-from-our-foreign-service-postsupdate/29954-ph-embassy-dot-partner-with-first-russian-female-michelin-chef-to-promote-filipino-cuisine-tourism

Department of Foreign Affairs (2021, February 26). ASEAN Embassies Partner in Promoting ASEAN Culture in 2021 Lao Food Festival. Retrieved March 5, 2023, fromhttps://dfa.gov.ph/dfa-news/news-from-our-foreign-service-postsupdate/2867 5-asean-embassies-partner-in-promoting-asean-culture-in-2021-lao-food-festival

Department of Foreign Affairs (2021, July 9). PH Participates in Annual International Food Festival in Vanuatu, Raises Funds for International Women's Group. Retrieved March 5, 2023, from https://dfa.gov.ph/gad-feature-news/29217-ph- participates-in-annual-international-food-festival-in-vanuatu-raises-funds-for-international-women-s-group

Department of Foreign Affairs (2021, June 17). Filipino Food Week Returns to Hawaii. Retrieved March 5, 2023, from https://dfa.gov.ph/dfa-news/news-from-our-foreign-service-postsupdate/29110-filipino-food-week-returns-to-hawaii

Department of Foreign Affairs (2021, May 28). PH Consulate General Toronto Zooms in on the Province of Batangas in "Conversations on the Province of Batangas and Filipino Cuisine". Retrieved March 5, 2023, from https://dfa.gov.ph/dfa-news/news-from-our-foreign-service-postsupdate/29022-ph-consulate-general-toronto-zooms-in-on-the-province-of-batangas-in-conversations-on-the-province-of-batangas-and-filipino-cuisine

Department of Foreign Affairs (2021, November 19). Visitors and Enterprises Flock to Food Philippines Pavilion at 4th China International Import Expo in Shanghai. Retrieved March 5, 2023, from https://dfa.gov.ph/dfa-news/news-from-our-foreign-service-postsupdate/29748-visitors-and-enter-prises-flock-to-foodphilippines-pavi lion-at-4th-china-international-im-port-expo-in-shanghai

Department of Foreign Affairs (2021, November 2). PH Agri-Food Products a Hit at the 2021 International Agriculture Exhibition in S. Korea. https://dfa.gov.ph/dfa-news/ news-from-our-foreign-service-postsupdate/29657-ph-agri-food-products-a-hit-at-the-2021-international-agriculture-exhibi-tion-in-s-korea

Department of Foreign Affairs (2021, September 20). Manila Comes to Town Food Truck Festival in Vancouver. Retrieved March 5, 2023, from https://dfa.gov.ph/dfa-news news-from-our-foreign-service-postsupdate/29476-manila-comes-to-town-food-truck-festival-in-vancouver

Department of Foreign Affairs (2022, April 7). FilAussie Women Advocate for Filipino Cuisine Celebrated in Book Launch of Under Coconut Skies. https://dfa.gov.ph gad-feature-news/30351-filaussie-women-advo-cate-for-filipino-cuisine-celebrated -in-book-launch-of-under-coconut-skies

Department of Foreign Affairs (2022, August 23). Philcongen Toronto Turns Over Flour Samples from Philippine Exporters to Local SMEs to Help Promote Philippine Cuisine and Products. Retrieved March 5, 2023, from https://dfa.gov.ph/ dfa-news/news-from-our-foreign-service-postsupdate/31044-philcongen-toronto-turns -over-flour-samples-from-philippine-exporters-to-local-smes-to-help-promote-phi lippine-cuisine-and-products

Department of Foreign Affairs (2022, November 22). Filipino Products Culture and Cuisine Showcased at the 5th Asean Festival in Kenya. Retrieved March 5, 2023, from https://dfa.gov.ph/dfa-news/news-from-our-foreign-service-postsupdate/313 89-filipino-products-culture-and-cuisine-showcased-at-the-5th-asean-festival-in-kenya

Department of Foreign Affairs (2022, November 28). PH Embassy in Washington, D.C., Highlights Culinary Achievements of Chef Evelyn Bunoan. Retrieved March 5, 2023, from https://dfa.gov.ph/dfa-news /news-from-our-foreign-service-posts update/31417-ph-embassy-in-washington-d-c-highlights-culinary-achievements-of-chef-evelyn-bunoan

Department of Foreign Affairs (2022, November 4). Alberta's Culinaire Magazine Features Filipino Cuisine in November. Retrieved March 5, 2023, from https://dfa ov.ph/dfa-news/news-from-our-foreign-service-postsupdate/31284-alberta-s-culinire-magazine-features-filipino-cuisine-in-november-2022-issue

Department of Foreign Affairs (2022, November 7). Filipino Community in Vanuatu Showcases PH Food International Festival. Retrieved March 5, 2023, from: https://dfa.gov.ph/dfa-news/news-from-our-foreign-service-postsupdate/31304-filipino-community-in-vanuatu-showcases-ph-food-international-festival

Department of Foreign Affairs (2022, October 27). Maritime Museum of Barcelona Showcases PH Cuisine in Fish in the Kitchens of the World. Retrieved March 5, 2023, from https://dfa.gov.ph/dfa-news/news-from-our-foreign-service-postsupdat e/31269-maritime-museum-of-barcelona-showcases-ph-cuisine-in-fish-in-the-kitc hens-of-the-world

Department of Foreign Affairs (n.d.). PH Consulate General in Milan attends #PhilippinesFoodTripping event. Retrieved March 9, 2023, from https:// dfa.gov.ph /dfa-news/news-from-our-foreign-service-postsupdate/29920-ph-consulate-genera l-in-milan-attends-philippinesfoodtripping-event.

Department of Foreign Affairs [Department of Foreign Affairs]. (2016, April 27). *PHL ambassador to Belgium calls for solidarity at St. Josse dinner event for Binalonan* [facebook post]. facebook. https://www.facebook.com/dfaphl/posts/pfbid06C78

Department of Tourism. (2018, November 16). *DOT statement on Madrid Fusion Manila*. Tourism Promotions Board Philippines. https://www.tpb.gov.ph/whats_new/dot-statement -on-madrid-fusion-manila-mfm/

Department of Tourism (2021, July 19). DOT Partner Agencies Celebrate Filipino Food Month. Retrieved March 5, 2023, from https://beta.tourism.gov.ph/news_and_updates/dot-partner-agencies-celebrate-filipino-food-month/

Department of Tourism (2022, April 6). DOT Backs Iloilo Bid for 'Creative City of Gastronomy' recognition from UNESCO. https://beta.tourism.gov.ph/news_and_updates/dot-backs-iloilo-bid-for-creative-city-of-gastronomy-recognition-from-unesco/

Department of Tourism (2022, June 10). DOT's KAIN NA! takes foodies to a multi-sensoryadventure.https://beta.tourism.gov.ph/news_and_updates/dots-kain-na-tak es-foodies-to-a-multi-sensory-adventure/

Department of Tourism (2023, March 15). DOT chief unveils National Tourism Development Plan (NTDP) 2023-2028 at stakeholders' summit. https://beta.tourism.gov.ph/news_and_updates/dot-chief-unveils-national-tourism-development-plan-ntdp-2023-2028-at-stakeholders-summit/

Department of Trade and Industry, (May, 2019). From trend to mainstream: PH rises in the world of food. Retrieved on: November 13, 2023 from: https://www.dti.gov.ph/archives/news-archives/from-trend-to-mainstream-ph-rises-in-the-world-of-food/

Department of Trade and Industry. (2020, January 14). *DTI-CITEM targets $22-m export deals in Taiwan food market.* Department of Trade and Industry Philippines.https:// www.dti.gov.ph/negosyo/exports/

Department of Trade and Industry. (n.d.). *Terms of Reference.* Department of Trade and Industry.

Department of Trade and Industry Philippines. (2022, November 23). *Ph active participation in 5th CIIE, showcases strength of the Philippines' food exports to China.* https://www.dti.gov.ph/overseas/shanghai/shanghai-news/ph-active-participation-in-5th-ciie-showcases-strength-of-the-philippines-food-exports-to-china/

Diplomat Magazine. (2017, May). *Kulinarya, a guide to Philippine food.* Diplomat Magazine. Retrieved March 7, 2023, from https://diplomatmagazine.eu/2017/05/20/kulina rya -guide-philippine-food/

DOT's Kain na! makes a comeback in Tagaytay - Love the Philippines! Welcome to the DOT's Corporate Site. (2022, May 6). Love the Philippines! Welcome to the DOT 's Corporate Site. https://beta.tourism.gov.ph/news_and_updates/dots-kain-na-ma kes-a-comeback-in- tagaytay/

Dunaway W. & Macabuac M.C., (October, 2022). *Globalized Food and Asian Hunger.* In Dunaway W. & Macabuac M.C., *Where Shrimp Eat Better than People* (pp. 124-165). Brill

Edo. (2020, September 26). Filipino Food Movement Australia presents "Sahog." E DeliciouS.https://e-deliciou-s.com/2020/02/19/filipino-food-movement-australia-present s-sahog/

Embassy of the Philippines, Berlin. (2015, June 25). *The Dayaw experience: A celebration of Filipino cuisine and volunteerism at Berlin food art week.* https://philippine-embassy.de/2015/06/25/the-dayaw-experience-a-celebration-of-filipino-cuisine-and-volunteerism-at-berlin-food-art-week/

Embassy of the Philippines, Berline (2015). Promoting the Philippines to German Communities: Embassy Officers Speak Before German and Filipino Groups. https://philippine-embassy.de/2015/09/15/promoting-the-philippines-to-german-communities-embassy-officers-speak-before-german-and-filipino-groups/

Embassy of the Philippines, Brasilia (n.d.). Philippine Foreign Policy. http://

philembassybrasilia.org/index.php/about-the-philippines/philippine-foreign-policy

Embassy of the Philippines, Doha, Qatar. (2015, September 3). *Kulinarya Qatar Officially Launched in Doha.* https://dohape.dfa.gov.ph/-kulinarya-qatar-officially-launched -in-doha

Embassy of the Philippines, Wellington, New Zealand. (2015). *Philippine embassy commends Auckland University of technology (AUT) and the Philippine honorary consulate general in Auckland for Filipino culinary delight.* https://embassy.org.nz/latest/news/philippine-embassy-commends-auckland-university-of-technology-aut-and-the-philippine-honorary-consulate-general-in-auckland-for-filipino-culinary-delight

Embassy of the Philippines Berlin. (2020, May 19). *Berlin PE Supports Community During Quarantine with Bayanihan Initiative.* The Philippine Embassy in Berlin. http://phil lippine-embassy.de/2020/05/19/berlin-pe-supports-community-during-quarintine-with-bayanihan-initiative/

Embassy of the Republic of the Philippines, Seoul (2021, April 27). PH Embassy in Seoul and Mama Sita Celebrate Filipino Food Month with Culinary Video Featuring Sinigang dish with Okra. http://www.philembassy-seoul.com/ann_detail. asp?id=12615

Embassy of the Republic of the Philippines, Tokyo (2022, February 1). Feature on Philippi ne Cuisine - Crosscut Asia. Retrieved March 5, 2023, from https://tokyo.philembassy.net/02news/feature-on-philippine-cuisine-crosscut-asia/

Filipino Food Movement Australia. (2018). *Meryenda Kape at Tsaa.* https://www.filipino foodmovementaustralia.org/meryenda-kape-at-tsaa

Fulton, A. (May, 2016). *Trend Watch: Filipino Food Heats Up.* Retrieved on: October 28, 2023 from: https://www.nationalgeographic.com/travel/article/filipino-food-trend- united-states

Golangco, L. (June, 2021). *Filipino Food—How Can We Go Further? Margarita Forés, Chele Gonzàlez, And More Speak Out.* Retrieved on: November 15, 2023 from: https://www.tatlerasia.com/dining/the-industry/filipino-food-how-can-we-go-even -further

Good News Filipinas Team, (September, 2017). *Philippines is the No. 1 tuna exporter to EU.* Retrieved on: October 28, 2023 from: https://www.goodnewspilipinas.com/philippines-no-1-tuna-exporter-eu/

Grana, R. (January, 2022). They toured the PH to study our heritage dishes—now they run one of the best restos in America. Retrieved on: November 15, 2023 from: https:// news.abs-cbn.com/ancx/food-drink/restaurants/01/06/22/filipino-resto-abac-in-sf-named-one-of-americas-best

Heritage Radio Network. (n.d.). *Amy Besa and Romy Dorotan.* Heritage Radio Network. (n.d.). https://heritageradionetwork.org/amy-besa-and-romy-dorotan

Inquirer.net US Bureau, (November, 2016). *Istorya-DC '16 spotlights Filipino cuisine, 'gastro-diplomacy'.* Retrieved on: November 15, 2023 from: https://globalnation.in quirer.net/148403/istorya-dc-16-spotlights-filipino-cuisine-gastro-diplomacy

Interface Tourism Spain. (2017, April 6). *Madrid Fusión Manila or How Gastronomy Is Key to Creating a Tourist Brand Interface Tourism.* Interface Tourism. https:/ /interfacetourism.es/en/2017/04/06/gastronomy-is-key-to-creating-a-tourist-brand/

Jay, S. (2020). *A Fil-Am Food Trip: Stories From Across The Pacific.* Tatler Asia. https://www.tatlerasia.com/dining/food/a-fil-am-food-trip-stories-from-across-the-pacific

Lariosa, S. (December, 2022). *Mark Wiens in Cebu: Here are the delectable dishes he tried in the 'Queen City of the South'.* Retrieved on: November 12, 2023 from: https://phil starlife.com/living/136606-mark-wiens-in-cebu?page=4

Lee, G. (2009). A theory of soft power and Korea's soft power strategy. *Korean Journal of Defense Analysis, 21*(2), 205-218. http://doi.org/10.1080/10163270902913962

Logarta, M. (April, 2018). *Filipino food is trending, thanks to Chef Gaita Fores.* Retrieved on: October 27, 2023 from: https://www.goodnewspilipinas.com/filipino-food-is-trending -thanks-to-chef-gaita-fores/

McNeilly, C. (June, 2017). How Filipino Food Is Becoming the Next Great American Cuisine. Retrieved on: November 13, 2023 from: https://www.vogue.com/article/ filipino-food -philippines -cuisine-restaurants

Melchor, J. (2016, June 2). *Petition for the celebration of buwan ng kulinaryang Pilipino.* Change.org.https://www.change.org/p/national-commission-for-culture-and-the-arts- petition-for-the-preservation-of-the-philippine-culinary-heritage-gastronomy

Mellejor, L. (2018, December 8). *PRRD wants DOT's 'Kaon Ta' to spice up PH as culinary destination.* Philippine News Agency. Retrieved March 12, 2023, from https://www.pna.gov.ph/articles/1056105

Mok, C. (April, 2017). Why The World Is Taking Notice Of Filipino Cuisine. Retrieved on: November 13, 2023 from: https://www.tatlerasia.com/dining/food/ph-why-the -world-is-taking-notice -of-filipino-cuisine

National Commission for Culture and the Arts. (n.d.). *Order of national artists.* https://nccagov.ph/about-culture-and-arts/culture-profile/national-artists-of-the-philippines/

Nirwandy, N., & Awang, A. A. (2014). Conceptualizing public diplomacy social conventi on culinary: Engaging gastro diplomacy warfare for economic branding. *Procedia-Social and Behavioral Sciences, 130*, 325-332.\

Nye, J. S. (2008). Public diplomacy and soft power. *The ANNALS of the American Academy of Political and Social Science, 616*(1), 94–109. https://doi.

org/10.1177/0002716207311699

Observer of Economic Complexity (2016). What does Philippines export? (2016). Retrieved on November 13, 2023 from: https://oec.world/en/visualize/tree_map /hs92/export /phl/all/show/2016

Philippine Embassy, Riyadh, (2015). *Phl Embassy in Riyadh Partners with Supermarket Giant to Promote Philippine Cuisine and Tourism. Facebook* https://tokyo.phil embassy.net/02news/philippine-embassy-in-japan-promotes-filipino-food-through-eats-more-fun-in-the-philippines-online-campaign/

Philippine Embassy in Cambodia. *Filipino Pizza Restaurant Chain "Yellow Cab".* (2020, February 11). Philippine Embassy – Tokyo, Japan. Retrieved March 14, 2023, from https://tokyo.philembassy.net/02news/philippine-embassy-in-japan-promotes-filip filipino-food-through-eats-more-fun-in-the-philippines-online-campaign/

PHL Embassy in Budapest participates in Diplomatic Fair 2012 | govph. (2012, December 6). Official Gazette of the Republic of the Philippines. https://www.officialgazette.gov.ph/2012/12/06/phl-embassy-in-budapest-participates-in-diplomatic-fair-2012/

Pornpongmetta, P., & Paribatra, P. (2019). *Gastrodiplomacy of Thailand, 1989-2019* (No. 180476). Thammasat University.

promotion. Philippine News Agency. Retrieved March 12, 2023, from https://www.pna. gov.ph/articles/1079228

Raimzhanova, A. (2015). Power In IR: Hard, Soft, and Smart Power. Ins https://doi.org/10.3726/b11642

Ramar Foods, (March, 2015). 5 Reasons Why Filipino Food is Emerging Trend in US. Retrieved on: November 13, 2023 from: https://www.manufacturing.net/home/news/13181033/ 5-reasons-why-filipino-food-is-emerging-trend-in-us

Regis, D. (March, 2023). *Kulinarya Qatar promotes Filipino cuisine with celebrity chef Niño Logarta.* Retrieved on October 27, 2023 from: https://www.qatar-tribune.com /article/56815/nation/kulinarya-qatar-promotes-filipino-cuisine-with-celebrity-chef-nino-logarta

Rocamora, A. L. (2018, January 25). *PH makes 'headway' as gastronomy hub in Asia*. Philippine News Agency. Retrieved March 12, 2023, from https://www.pna.gov.ph /articles/1022866

Rocamora, A. L. (2019, September 1). *Luring tourists through Filipino food, flavors*. Philippine News Agency. Retrieved March 12, 2023, from https://www.pna.gov.ph /articles/1079248

Rocamora, A. L. (2022, October 18). *France, PH highlight 'diversity' in 75th year of diplomatic ties.* Philippine News Agency. Retrieved March 14, 2023, from https://w ww.pna.gov.ph /articles/1186471

Roces, M. (November, 2021). *Filipino migrants are agents of change.* Retrieved on November 20, 2023 from: https://www.lowyinstitute.org/the-interpreter/filipino -migrants-are-agents-change

Rockower, P. (2012). Recipes for gastrodiplomacy. *Place Branding and PublicDiplomacy, 8*(3), 235-246.

Romualdez, B. (2019, July 27). *DC Pinoy Food Festival*. Philstar.com; Philstar. com. https://www.philstar.com/lifestyle/allure/2019/07/28/1938411/dc-pinoy-food-festival

S. No. 244: Providing for the development and preservation of Philippine culinary heritage [Philippines], 11 July, 2022, available at: https://legacy.senate.gov.ph/lis/bill/_res. aspx?congress=18&q=SBN244

Sicat, A. (August, 2023). *WOFEX Manila 2023: Biggest food trade show in the PH is back!* Retrieved on October 27, 2023 from: https://pia.gov.ph/news/2023/08/02 /wofex-manila- 2023-biggest-food-trade-show-in-the-ph-is-back

Tagala, D. (June, 2018). *Couple opened Filipino resto in U.S. after encouraged by Antho ny Bourdain.* Retrieved on: November 21, 2023 from: https://news.abs-cbn.com/life/06/16/18/couple-opened-filipino-resto-in-us-after-encouraged-by-anthony-bo urdain

Tayag, C. (2016, July 20). *Inspired by chef Anna Olson*. Philstar.com; Philstar.com. https://www.philstar.com/lifestyle/food-and-leisure/2016/07/21/1604844/inspired-chef-anna-olson

The Filipino Food Movement. (n.d.). Press. Filipino Food Movement. https://filipinofood movement.weebly.com/press.html

Tiu, C. (2014). *Madrid Fusion 2015: Putting Philippine Cuisine on the Global Map.* Forbes. Retrieved November 15, 2023, from https://www.forbes.com/sites/cheryltiu/2014/12/29/madrid-fusion-2015-putting-philippine-cuisine-on-the-global-map/? sh=6e4d29aa62e5

Tunay, Z. (September, 2022). *Kulinarya Qatar 2022 is Back with their Food, Culture and Trade Festival this October!.* Retrieved on October 27, 2023 from: https://bestlifeq atar.com/2022/09/29/kulinarya-qatar-2020-is-back/

Unite, B. (November, 2021). PH agri products gain attention from South Koreans in agri exhibition. Retrieved on November 12, 2023 from: https://mb.com.ph/2021/11/02/ph-agri-products-gain -attention-from-south-koreans-in-agri-exhibition

Vergara, K.Y. (March, 2023). *#PreserveFilipinoFood: DA leads Filipino Food Month 2023 celebration.* Retrieved on October 27, 2023 from: https://www.da. gov. ph/preservefilipinofood-da-leads-filipino-food-month-2023-celebration/

Vicencio-Luz, K. (September, 2022). *Filipino cuisine elevated to greater heights.* Retrieved on: October 28, 2023 from: https://www.philippine-embassy.org.sg /filipino-cuisin e-elevated-to-greater-heights/

Visaya, M. G. (2021, August 19). *'Experience a Taste of the Philippines': Filipino*

Restaurant Week returns from August 18 to 27 — Life Eastyle Magazine. Asian Journal. Retrieved March 14, 2023,from https://www.asianjournal. com/magazine s/life-eastyle-magazine/experience-a-taste-of-the-philippines-filipino-restaurant-week-returns-from-august-18-to-27/

White, W., Barreda A., Hein S. (2019). Gastrodiplomacy: Captivating a global audience through cultural cuisine - A systematic review of the literature. *Journal of Tourismology* 5(2), 127-144. https://doi.org/10.26650/jot.2019.5.2.0027.

Yadao, L., & Irene. (2015, November 25). *Off the menu: Asian America*. Off the Menu AsianAmerica.https://caamedia.org/offthemenu/2015/11/23/amy-besa-the-trail blazer/

Zubiri, S. (November, 2021). Filipino cuisine isn't as well-known as other Asian foods — but that's changing. Retrieved on: November 13, 2023 from: https://www.cnbc.com/2021/11/22/what-is-filipino-food-and-what-does-it-taste-like-chefs-explain.html

Chapter 2

A Hybrid Ballgame:
Analyzing Philippine Basketball and Cultural Identity on the Hard Court of American Hegemony*

Jaecian Onoh A. Cesar, Danika Maria Sandra B. Corias, Nayeli Jane T. Jusa, & Frances Victoria D. Magallanes

ABSTRACT

Basketball is one of the most enduring cultural legacies of American colonialism in the Philippines. While Filipinos have essentially owned the sport by fusing their local styles, values, and contexts with American standards, gameplays, and mentalities in the sport, the resulting hybridity of Philippine basketball remains overshadowed by the stark cultural influence of American basketball in the country. Extant literature falls short in extensively discussing the factors and reasons behind the sustained relevance of colonial-rooted sports like basketball and their implications in forming the sports cultural identities within contemporary societies. Hence, it is imperative to investigate the perpetuation and continued acceptance of American basketball among Filipino enthusiasts and how such dynamics hone the present basketball culture in the country. This study grounded Homi Bhabha's concept of Hybridity in scrutinizing the current Philippine basketball culture vis-à-vis the American culture. Findings showed that American exceptionalism, capitalism, and preference for masculine body ideals pervade Philippine basketball. Filipinos continue to accept these American influences because of the sport's perceived social and economic opportunities. Furthermore, findings revealed that Filipino enthusiasts' continued acceptance of American basketball hybridizes contemporary Philippine basketball when ascribed to Filipino values, ideas, and narratives in the practice of the sport, as well as through their demands for systemic reform concerning the sporting development in the country. The study concluded that the continuous intermingling of American and Philippine basketball cultures creates an ambivalent hybrid basketball culture. Such ambivalence explains the persistent significance of Americanized basketball in the Philippines and the complex dynamics that define Filipino sporting cultural identity.

Keywords: *Philippine basketball culture, hybridity, ambivalence, cultural identity*

*Awarded as Best Thesis
for AB International Studies Major in American Studies (2024).*

Introduction

For many societies today, modern sports are tightly woven into their histories of colonialism under Western imperial powers. As Western colonialism gradually ended in the 20th century, the various sports introduced by the colonizers remained deeply entrenched in their formerly colonized societies. It is noteworthy that most sporting cultures continue to perpetuate and reinforce Western perspectives on how people shape and view their bodies, live a particular lifestyle, conform to gender roles, and craft meaningful structure and purpose to their lives (Cleophas, 2021; Sosis & Kiper, 2022). Hence, modern sports are concrete legacies of colonization, serving as a terrain upon which postcolonial identities and relations are expressed, contested, and reconstructed (Bale & Cronin, 2003; Horton, 2011).

Filipinos' affinity with modern sports can be traced back to American colonialism. During those times, sports were used to transmit American cultural practices, ideas, values, and norms to their Filipino subjects (Gems, 2016). Sports aimed to not only assimilate Filipinos with American culture but also to help them veer away from their supposed "backwardness" by adopting principles and social codes necessary for national self-determination and "fitness" for democracy (Huebner, 2013). As a result of the deepening Filipino-American relations during and after the colonial era, basketball eventually became the most popular sport and claimed a prominent position in the broader Philippine sporting culture.

Interestingly, the hegemonic status of basketball in the Philippines parallels the position occupied by the United States in the Philippines. The Americans' legacy may never be absolute, but their imprint on the Philippine cultural landscape pervades at large (Antolihao, 2015). Although the ubiquity of basketball can be explained from the lens of the liberal internationalist perspective that today's sporting industry is commonly predicated on, the broader picture leaves out the unequal power dynamics at play within the convergence of cultures. As such, the Filipinos' relative success in embracing basketball, as evidenced by the extent of their technical imprints on the sport, has also been a nagging source of frustration and disappointment at present. In other words, the problems, issues, and controversies hounding the present Philippine basketball landscape arise when the dominant sport remains rooted in an American sporting culture that extols ideals and opportunities that disproportionately favor American standards and rationalities.

A comprehensive review of the literature revealed that there is a rich and established scholarly consensus on the role of sports in the Western imperial project, the inseparability of sports and nationalism, and the contradicting notions of the inclusive and exclusive nature of the global sporting industry (Gems, 2016; Antolihao, 2015; Hubner, 2013, 2016; Giulianotti, 2015). However, such scholarship failed to scrutinize the abiding coloniality of some sports and how such coloniality is sustained and internalized, and how it has honed the sport cultural identities of postcolonial societies. The scarcity of such scholarly undertaking is pronounced in the Philippine context. Extant literature falls short in analyzing the factors and reasons why a popular colonial-rooted sport like basketball continues to be perpetuated and accepted among Filipinos, despite the constant pitfalls and contentions hounding the sport at present. More importantly, the dearth of research fails to build on a more nuanced understanding of how the massive American basketball influence, coupled with local Filipino contexts, ideas, and norms, shapes the present Filipino sport cultural identity. To grapple with such gaps, the study aimed to determine the influential elements of American basketball culture in the Philippines, understand why Filipino basketball enthusiasts accept such influence, and elucidate how such influences are hybridized in Philippine contexts.

This study is anchored on Homi Bhabha's concept of hybridity, elucidated in his book The Location of Culture (1994). Hybridity refers to the development of new transcultural forms within the colonial engagement or the contact of the colonizer with the colonized Other (Bhabha, 1994). Within hybridity is the "in-between space" or the third space where the negotiations of culture and identity between the colonizer and colonized happen, resulting in cultural hybridity. In simultaneous with such cultural contact is the process of mimicry, where the colonized Other "imitates" the colonizer. This imitation becomes the colonized Other's representation and sign of indeterminacy. Therefore, the pursuit of the transformed Other, being the ones that were colonized is seen as "a difference that is almost the same but not quite" (Bhabha, 1994). Therefore, these processes facilitate ambivalence, allowing both the subversion and reinforcement of the colonizer and colonized Others' culture and identity. Ambivalence in this aspect describes the fluctuating process of exaltation and repulsion of the colonized Other to the colonial power (Mambrol, 2017). Reinforcement in the third space pertains to certain ideas, practices, norms, and values used to benefit and revere both the colonizer and the colonized Other. Subversion, on the other hand, is the disavowal of particular ideas, practices, norms, and values that are not beneficial or are considered to be undesirable.

The study, therefore, contributes to the understanding that the Philippine basketball culture is hybrid in character. The hybridity of Philippine basketball can be characterized first by the extensive aspects of American basketball that pervade in the Philippines. Many Filipino basketball enthusiasts then internalize these wide-ranging influences. The broad influence of American basketball, coupled with local Filipino ideational concepts and practical demands for developing the sport, further hybridizes basketball. Simultaneously present within such factors, reasons, and processes in the hybridization of Philippine basketball are the instances of mimicry, reinforcement, and subversion. The study is limited to studying the sport of basketball in the Philippine context and uses a qualitative research design to identify Filipino basketball enthusiasts' perceptions, practices, and experiences in analyzing the Philippine culture's hybridity. Information is taken from interviews with Filipino basketball enthusiasts, such as the players, coaches, officials, media practitioners, and fans actively involved in basketball. The secondary data source was from documentary and multimedia sources. The study used purposive and snowball sampling methods to select the participants and deductive thematic analysis to analyze the obtained data.

The Pervading Elements of American Basketball Culture

The extent of American basketball's influence in the Philippines can be attributed firstly to the widespread exceptionalist view of American basketball, as evidenced by the National Basketball Association's (NBA) dominance and gameplay standards. Second, there is a robust capitalist ethos in Philippine basketball, given the steep commercialization and the culture of consumerism present among Filipino basketball enthusiasts. Third, there are prevailing exclusivist practices that enable the cultivation of certain physical biases, asymmetrical gender representation, and racialized ideas about the game of basketball.

There is a rich discourse pertaining to American exceptionalism in Philippine basketball. Conceptually, it is the belief that the USA is an extraordinary nation that has a special role in human history—a nation that is not just unique, but also superior (Aiello, 2022). When contextualized to sports, American exceptionalism manifests in how American sports, like basketball, carry and propagate ideas that exalt the unique qualities of the American identity (Gems & Pfister, 2009). The sentiments and perceptions of the study's participants pertained that the NBA, as a league that presents and produces the world's top basketball talent, is "the standard" that all basketball institutions and players in the world must aspire to be. Such a standard is rooted in the common belief among Filipino basketball enthusiasts: American basketball is the most superior basketball culture today.

The popularity of basketball in the Philippines can be credited mainly to the NBA's extensive reach to its Filipino viewers. Research participants expressed that the NBA players' sheer physicality, talent, and the ability to perform well-executed plays, allows the league to draw a larger audience who will closely follow the league and its players. The NBA's global initiatives aim to expand and diversify its fan base through activities like the NBA Global Games and Basketball Without Borders (Fuertes Jr., 2024). These initiatives have also found their way to the Philippines, strategically positioning NBA players internationally. The advent of social media has also prompted the NBA to emphasize the social media presence of its players—providing glimpses into the personal lives of the athletes and effectively humanizing them. Such multifaceted strategies have successfully broadened the appeal of NBA players and effectively cemented their place in the hearts of Filipino basketball enthusiasts.

Participants also stressed that while the rest of the world is catching up with the American style of basketball, they acknowledge that no other basketball league can match the standard and quality that the NBA has pioneered all these years. For them, the NBA has established itself as the epitome of what a basketball league ought to be—showcasing exceptionally skilled players, entertaining gameplays, and an indelible global presence. This elevated standard is attributed to several key elements, including the league's commitment to investing in their athletes by continually providing them with state-of-the-art training facilities and employing highly qualified coaches. The NBA also invests in high production values in the market, ensuring their broadcast quality and engaging content (Widjaya, 2024). All these efforts to ensure that their athletes are at the top of their game and that the gameplay is properly broadcasted set the NBA to become the benchmark for basketball leagues globally.

The prevalence of the NBA in the Philippines also influences how Filipinos play basketball, thus encouraging many to follow suit with the gameplay that NBA players practice, display, and promote. The American style of basketball is characterized by several key elements supposedly "distinct" among American teams (Huffman, 2023). For one, the fast break style, elevator screenplays, and hammer plays are among the offensive maneuvers that American teams have extensively developed. The American style of gameplay is also known for maximizing individual potential by crafting structured offensive plays and utilizing specific players to create opportunities for scoring. Therefore, Americans highly value exceptionally talented individual players who boast superior athleticism and are capable of dominating the court and being the team's star player.

Due to the appeal of the American basketball gameplay and the charm of star players, Filipinos would attempt to copy such gameplay and try to suit it by their means. Given the lack of players who possess the needed height, athletic built, and adequate exposure to dominate the game of basketball, there is a tendency for Filipinos to admire and then copy offensive and defensive sequences practiced in the NBA, like slam dunks, smooth three-point shooting, layups, and other impeccable offensive and defensive sequences. Sai (personal communication, September 17, 2023), a basketball coach, emphasized that the "American way" of basketball has long been ingrained in the basketball culture in the Philippines and is revered by many Filipinos. Filipino basketball athletes and coaches would try to follow their idols, believing that nobody can be on par with them, or in other words, they are the "cream of the crop." Jess (personal communication, October 8, 2023), a collegiate basketball coach and a semi-pro player, elaborated that American basketball players and teams have been widely recognized for employing "individualistic" tactics when playing the game. This means that teams mostly rely on the individual actions of players and for a single player to carry the load in one aspect of the game, either defensively or offensively. Indeed, the standards set by the NBA have continually reinforced the building blocks of the Philippines' basketball culture, especially on how the sport is practiced from a physical and strategic standpoint. For a long time, Filipinos have drawn inspiration from the NBA and have tried to reach the standards that the NBA has established.

Data also indicated that the American basketball culture manifests itself through capitalism in the Philippine basketball scene. With the NBA's influence on the professionalization of basketball in the Philippines in the 1970s, it has also laid the groundwork for the sport to cater to a thriving domestic and global sporting business industry. In the context of Philippine basketball, the country's professional basketball leagues have undergone a significant shift due to the influence of the explosive growth of American show business and the global impact of audio-visual mass media. The advent of the Philippine Basketball Association (PBA) in 1975, which was primarily inspired and copied from the NBA, created inroads for the "play for pay" setup that many Filipino ballers have widely adopted; the term roughly means that one gets to be paid in exchange for playing basketball (Antolihao, 2016). Specifically, Philippine basketball games feature more entertainment components and celebrity involvement.

Commercial interests are the prime driving forces behind the top basketball leagues in the Philippines. Comparing specifically the NBA and the PBA, participants stated that even though the leagues differ in how teams represent themselves as "brands"—cities in the NBA, while companies in the PBA—both are inherently profit-based, hence the term "franchise" and aim to not just sell basketball as a mere spectacle of entertainment and physical prowess, but also a show of corporate strength. The Philippine basketball industry is also well into integrating modes of advertising like the ones practiced in the US. The rise of online streaming platforms for watching basketball games, such as the NBA League Pass, paved the way for similar lucrative subscription and streaming on-demand deals and social media advertising in the Philippines. These are a step further than the traditional modes of corporatism that the Philippine basketball industry used to rely on, such as solely conducting multi-million-peso broadcast rights deals and the timeout and half-time commercial revenues. The rise of Filipino-based video-on-demand platforms allows one to access many live-streamed games from the NBA, PBA, the UAAP, or even the international tournaments in which the Gilas Pilipinas national team competes (Leongson, 2022).

Despite all the benefits associated with basketball's profitability, some participants lamented that the strong emphasis on money-making in Philippine basketball might somehow impact the quality of the game. For most participants in this study, the significance placed on profits might curtail the evenness of talent and competitiveness among teams, which also affects how audiences perceive the thrill they expect in a supposedly high-level competition. This apparent financial disparity in the capability to acquire highly skilled players can significantly impact the game's competitive balance, the intensity of fan engagement, and the overall capability of a team to last in the basketball scene.

Given all these, it is worth noting that profits and revenues indeed sustain the Philippine basketball industry, mainly that leagues, teams, and players rely on the financial support companies give them in exchange for marketing and advertising their products or services. Unsurprisingly, revenues are strongly considered in Philippine basketball when organizing formal and elite-level tournaments. After all, spectator sports like basketball bring prestige to the status of a significant player in the network industry and attract loyal and predictable audiences who need media coverage to gain expertise and be part of the fan community (Downey, 2001 & Mondello, 2006). It is, therefore, crucial to understand that the emphasis on the money-making facet of basketball is also a prime contributor to fostering the culture of consumerism and commodification among the Filipino basketball clientele.

Commodification is also rampant in Philippine basketball. Vamplew (2019) argues that "sport becomes a commodity when either consumers are willing to pay to play or watch it or if it has a potential exchange value rather than merely a use one." Much of this sports consumer behavior is rooted in what Funk et al. (2008) argue as the individuals' desire to seek an experience that satisfies their internal needs and then obtain its associated benefits. In the Philippines, the booming profitability of basketball expands its market share of consumers towards other industries as well. With the dominance of the NBA in the global basketball scene, it is worth noting how the league's expansive pioneering and innovation in marketing shapes the same processes among the consumer cultures that participate in the sport, especially Filipinos.

Exemplifying such consumer behavior is Claud (personal communication, September 8, 2023), an avid fan of the sport since her childhood, who shared that buying some of the products that her basketball idols endorse completely creates a different kind of experience and connection with the players she admires. A confessed Stephen Curry fan, Claud said that having a jersey replica of the sharpshooter from the Golden State Warriors makes her feel as if she has a piece of who Curry is, let alone make her feel like she is one with the team's highs and lows even though they are miles away from her. She said, *"Satisfaction talaga ito ng fans, na feel mo na andun ka din, nakaka-relate ka sa idols mo, lalo na sa jerseys kahit na mahal."* (It is definitely satisfying for fans to feel that you are one with your idols, especially having their jersey, no matter how expensive they are.)

As a deeply entrenched commercial enterprise, sports practitioners commodify themselves in a logic that also centers on making themselves "profitable" (Sullivan, 2006). Indeed, it is shared among all interviewees, especially athletes, to say that being marketable would mean that one must be a stellar player with high-level skills. For a pro athlete like Andrei (personal communication, September 13, 2023), having an impressive winning record makes one standout and more noticeable for brand endorsers. Coming from a famous college team with a vast fan and alumni community, he considered his accomplishments in high school and college to have enabled him to be at the receiving end of incentives from various league and team sponsors. All these have inclined him to be more marketable than his peers who did not have as many resources and impressive track record as he had. Most interviewees in this study concur that such a capitalist basis is an influential tool for the Philippine basketball industry's operations and is, therefore, necessary for basketball to thrive. Hence, such an influence motivates them to engage with the sport continually.

The globalization of American basketball, fueled by the media's role in massive reach and the institutionalization of the NBA in the Philippine popular culture, has also significantly influenced the biases among Filipino basketball players and enthusiasts. While physical attributes are often considered advantageous for professional players, research indicates that comparing strength traits and jumping ability is an inadequate and discriminative factor among professional athletes (Koklu et al., 2011 & Sallet et al., 2005). Athletic training can improve an athlete's speed, agility, and weight. Ultimately, consistent training can overcome shortcomings in one's natural prowess, just as it can in the world of basketball or any other sport (Berri et al., 2005). However, the data collected by the researchers indicated the presence of physical biases among both current and aspiring basketball athletes in engaging in the sport.

For example, Josiah, a coach in a private basketball camp, added, "In the Philippines, we are one of the most skilled players, but [in terms of] athleticism, not so much" (personal communication, September 8, 2023). Although talent and athleticism are not mutually exclusive, they are the two attributes basketball athletes must ideally possess to become well-rounded players. A professional player, Allan (personal communication, September 13, 2023), also agreed that height is an inherent advantage in basketball, which cannot be coached or taught, unlike some skills. He, along with most of the research participants, said that "Height is might," showing more significant preferential bias and deference towards those with the height advantage and emphasizing that there is no amount of training that could surpass the advantage of someone who is already tall. Indeed, the globalization of the NBA may have helped elevate the sporting institution as one of the channels of liberal and democratic values. However, it also cannot be denied how the sheer extent of such appeal also inadvertently reinforced physical biases that continually influenced the game's structure.

More than the physical aspects, biases in basketball also intersect with gender, thereby dichotomizing who gets to participate and enjoy the limelight in the sport. Most of the participants in this study perceived basketball primarily as a "masculine" sport, ideally aimed towards the participation and consumption of mostly men. Philippine basketball, as influenced by the dominance of the NBA—a league for men—also perpetuates such a form of patriarchal dominance. For instance, Miguel (personal communication, September 13, 2023), a basketball enthusiast, argued that genetics-wise, "men are more athletic and physically stronger than women," which is why it is understandable that basketball is a male-dominated sport. Certainly, there is an underlying double standard among Philippine basketball players, especially towards female athletes. The perception of basketball of being a sport primarily for men can be attributed mainly to the media's presentation of the sport. Leagues for men are usually the ones that are given the most press coverage and advertisement and are well-attended by the public.

Additionally, despite efforts to demonstrate that female ballers are just as capable as their male counterparts and dispel any doubts about their ability to play the game, they still have to conform to how society views women. Aiello (2023) stated that to persuade the basketball enthusiast that participating in basketball leagues is a professional activity, female basketball players must play tough basketball while observing the politics of gendered respectability off the court. For instance, female participants in the study agreed that they needed to appear and dress in a specific way when playing basketball to meet societal standards of what constitutes a woman, even in basketball. Jaimee (personal communication, September 20, 2023), a semi-professional athlete, full-time coach, and former collegiate basketball player, shared that during her time playing for one of the top universities in the Philippines, female varsity members were compelled to constantly keep their hair long so that they can be better perceived as "*babae jud*" (real woman). The asymmetrical representation in Philippine basketball is manifested at least in terms of media coverage, corporate investment, and gate attendance—proving that "breaking the glass ceiling" remains an elusive goal for many female athletes in basketball.

The human physique has also been an avenue for exemplifying 'racial difference' to promote the white masculine culture, dividing people and fostering notions of superiority and inferiority based on race and skin color (Aquino, 2015). Consequently, this fosters a surface-level tolerance for athletes, especially black athletes, who possess innate talent and physical endowment in athleticism (Buras, 2002). Likewise, statements from the research participants reflect an internalized belief that they would never prevail against foreigners in the sport, particularly those of African descent, in terms of genetics, often using terms like "*mga negro*" to refer to most of the basketball players in the PBA and the "imports" who get to be acquired by collegiate teams in the Philippines.

Cases of racial prejudice have manifested an absurd sense of superiority in Filipino basketball enthusiasts over black athletes due to their subconscious efforts to perpetuate the dominant white narrative. Van Van (personal communication, September 16, 2023), a participant in the study, expressed that they had less regard for foreign players, particularly black athletes, despite their physical superiority. After contrasting the physical bodies of Filipino players with the American black athletes, one participant even felt the need to claim that these black athletes have a distinct scent associated with them. This claim is a subtle denigration of foreign black players. Following Mignolo (2009), the cause of perceivable and elusive racism today, if context ualized in Philippine basketball, is a consequence of the Western viewpoints and interests that have been ingrained in Filipino minds and practices, which caused such notions of racial bias to be accepted as normal.

The data gathered showed that biases are pervasive in Philippine basketball, a fact that is strongly related to American colonialism's influence and the development of basketball as a modern sport. A few Filipino basketball enthusiasts consciously emulated and mimicked American and American basketball practices, along with prejudiced perceptions in the aspect of tallness and physicality, gender, and race. The emulation of these biases is primarily driven by their implicit desire to uphold American standards in the game while simultaneously engaging in subtle critiques of these practices.

Taking all of these into account, the American basketball culture perpetuates in Philippine basketball through a complex nexus of discourses that explicitly and implicitly position the American style of basketball in high regard. The American exceptionalist, capitalist, and exclusivist discourses circumscribe how basketball in the Philippines is perceived and practiced by those who engage closely with the sport. Data revealed that, fundamentally, those who engage in basketball tend to emulate American basketball's standards, practices, and norms, effectively determining the sport's structure and stylistics, commercial nature, and "ideal" participants in Philippine basketball. American exceptionalism captures most interviewees' prevailing ideas and perceptions of the American basketball culture—that the United States is metaphorically in a different league. Filipino basketball enthusiasts recognize the primacy of the United States' dominating, innovative, and competitive athletic pedigree in the sport, associating primarily with the NBA and the values and ideas its players explicitly and implicitly propagate. Moreover, the nexus between basketball, the media, and commercial interests gives more depth to how the American basketball culture ingrained itself in the Philippines. Additionally, exclusivist preferences sustain the American basketball culture in the Philippines. Participants affirmed the notion that the sport favors and caters to people with specific attributes only, most of which are rooted in a racialized and gendered understanding of physical bodies.

The Filipinos' Internalization of American Basketball Culture

Filipino enthusiasts remain closely engaged in the sport as they have internalized American basketball culture. Firstly, many Filipinos do not consciously regard the American basketball culture as something detrimental or overtly at play in their affection for the sport, in the sense that simply engaging in basketball induces a profound personal affect on themselves. Furthermore, it is a common viewpoint that basketball is a valuable tool to achieve upward social mobility, emphasizing economic opportunities and extensive social connections one can access when engaging in the sport.

There is a consensus in many empirical studies in the sociology of sports that many factors, such as physical characteristics, socioeconomic status, and geographical location, push individuals and groups to indulge in a specific sport (Giulianotti, 2015). Among these factors is *affect*, which simply refers to when one experiences feelings and emotions (Watson et al., 1992). As a fundamental component of an individual's experience, *affect* is an influential factor in many sporting contexts, such as in the identification with a team or player and personal grit and motivation to engage in the sport, supported by their family and peers.

For many, families and peers play a critical role in determining sports participation, exemplifying empirical research that one's immediate social environment greatly determines exposure to sports. Such relations, particularly familial ties, create the most accessible form of role models that individuals emulate and look up to. A big part of bolstering this relationship is that families across many residential communities in the Philippines find easy access to basketball courts that offer immediate spaces for the individuals' families and peers to play the game (Divinagracia, 2020). For example, Jaimee, a professional women's basketball athlete and a full-time high school coach, shared that realizing her father's dream of becoming a professional player gives her a different sense of fulfillment, which urged her to work harder in order to win championships and finish college with flying colors to make her parents proud.

In addition, there are those who had been influenced by their peers to engage in basketball. Most, if not all, agree that having peers like one's classmates, neighbors, churchmates, and workmates definitely enriches one's interest in the sport. Vladimir, a basketball fan, said that it is way more enjoyable to have peers with the same interests as him, stressing that having people on the same page as him somehow confers a sense of being understood (personal communication, October 7, 2023).

Furthermore, basketball players do not merely display and project their physical skills since they embody their values and mindsets. Hence, many Filipino basketball enthusiasts identify and view themselves with a few successful basketball stars they admire both internationally and locally. Kobe, one of the basketball media practitioners interviewed by the researchers, said that his father named him after the legendary Los Angeles Lakers cager Kobe Bryant. Kobe Bryant, along with other stars like Michael Jordan and LeBron James, to name a few, increased people's interest in basketball on the world stage. Kobe Bryant was known for his skills and talent, but his "Mamba mentality" captured many fans worldwide.

The "Mamba effect" has significantly influenced the Filipino hoops community, as it continues to inspire enthusiasts to ignite their love for basketball, which, for many people, has no bounds. For his part, Kobe (personal communication, September 15, 2023) lived by the legacy of his namesake. He shared that even as a kid, he already had this awareness to approach basketball, and indeed his life, like Kobe's—one that never settles for less. Hence, when Kobe Bryant died in 2020, Kobe (personal communication, September 15, 2023) felt as if something had also died in him. Andrei, a professional player who personally met and played with Kobe Bryant, shared that such a competitive mindset aided him and his teams win several high school and college championships. He added that the winning tradition he has gotten used to has become "addicting." For Sai, this hunger for winning and success is best exemplified by the resourcefulness of many Filipino players, stating that many Filipinos play on makeshift courts or even without proper equipment. (personal communication, September 17, 2023).

It is interesting to note that the players they admire usually come from modest socioeconomic backgrounds and gritty personal characteristics. Internationally, they commonly mention the likes of Kobe Bryant, Stephen Curry, Lebron James, and Michael Jordan—all NBA stars in different generations, and all share a "rags to riches" story. Domestically, they also have diverse answers about who they admire; most mentioned is Jun Mar Fajardo, a multi-titled, multi-Most Valuable Player awardee, and other Gilas Pilipinas players. Many resonate with Jun Mar's humble beginnings and colorful journey to stardom in the Philippine basketball scene.

One of the prevailing reasons why Filipinos internalize American basketball influences is the appeal of climbing the socioeconomic ladder. Social mobility refers to how people will likely move up or down within life's economic or social ladder (Eyles et al., 2022). Participants in this study positioned themselves in an upward social mobility when engaging in basketball. From a functionalist perspective, social mobility in sports can be achieved directly and indirectly (Delaney, 2015). The direct ways can be in the form of participating in professional sports. In contrast, indirect ways can be used to earn sports scholarships, which predisposes athletes to better job opportunities (Delaney, 2015). Advancing in life is a strong motivation and carries much appeal to those who wish to use basketball as a venue for opening new and better opportunities for themselves, especially among Filipino basketball enthusiasts who come from the lower rungs of the socioeconomic ladder. Most Filipinos view this socioeconomic advancement positively, indicating that American influence benignly impacts Filipinos' preference for basketball.

For most of the participants in this study, economic opportunities are inseparable from basketball. As discussed, the professionalization of the sport in the country opened doors for economic progress for large business entities and those who engage with the sport, especially the athletes themselves. Most participants in this study have been student-athletes or casual players in community-level tournaments. For example, Allan (personal communication, September 13, 2023) primarily credited basketball for the economic opportunities he has been reaping since elementary school. Now earning a decent salary as a professional club player, Allan had been on a full athletic scholarship under his school's varsity teams. From high school to grad school, Allan's middle-class parents never spent a single peso for his tuition and sporting expenses, which he thought was advantageous for him to focus solely on his studies. Along these lines, Allan has reaped the comforts provided by the direct and indirect pathways of economic mobility—direct, from the ample salary he gets in the pro ranks, and indirect for obtaining high educational achievements, which he said he can make use of should he ever decide to quit basketball.

Most participants stressed that all the athletes' efforts must also be rewarded, and monetary incentives like salaries and bonuses are their inevitable end goals. Francis, a coach and a league organizer (personal communication, October 14, 2023), contended that athletic careers have shelf lives. This means one can only reach the apex of athletic performance and conditioning at a certain point. Hence, younger players offered to play overseas should not lose that chance. For him, Philippine leagues and teams should not hamper Filipino players from chasing their dreams wherever it may take them. In the Philippines, professional basketball players, specifically those who are in a prominent league like the PBA, earn salaries capped from Php 50,000 up to Php 420,000 per month, which is around Php 1.8 million to Php 5 million per season, depending on the player's category (PBA Updates, 2023). For those who are acquired by foreign teams like in the Korean Basketball League (KBL) and the Japan Basketball League (JBL), players can earn as much as Php 4 million to Php 9 million from signing deals alone (Leongson, 2022 & Ganglani, 2021).

However, the centrality of basketball's profit-making purpose may also serve adverse practices in the industry. For example, the desire to earn money in basketball leads one to play dirty; some athletes, coaches, and organizers resort to "game fixing," which is the act of playing or officiating matches with predetermined results, motivated by gambling and lucrative financial transfers. Van (personal communication, September 16, 2023), a community league organizer and a player who frequently plays for barangay tournaments, commented that while he abhors the cheating incidences, he otherwise does not judge those "nagabaligya og dula" or those who sell their game for the sake of money—understanding how poverty makes one desperate for money. Nevertheless, he remains adamant on his stand that game-fixing is unethical; as a player, one should embody good skills and qualities, showing one's best without under-the-table transactions. He adds that it affects the younger fans negatively. Their advantage is that in-game fixing, their pay doubles. He further stated that some games quickly get boring because of game fixing.

Other than the economic prospects, most Filipino basketball enthusiasts used their sport to expand their social networks. This is exemplified by how they acquire personal support and fellowship with other individuals, embedding themselves in their respective communities. These, in turn, cultivate a sense of recognition and enable the exchange of material and social support. Janelle, a collegiate varsity player, shared that even if her team does not win any match, it would still be a win for her as long as she has created meaningful interactions with the people she gets to play against (personal communication, September 18, 2023). Additionally, through basketball, many are given scholarship opportunities in many prominent universities in the Philippines. Francis (personal communication, October 14, 2023), a local league organizer, expressed:

> *On the financial level, before ako nag start [nitong liga na ito], wala na ako masyadong mga friends. But because of basketball, marami [akong] mga nakilala. Naging malaki ang network ko and nagkaroon ako ng mas maraming business prospects.*

> (On the financial level, before I started this league, I no longer had that many friends. But, because of basketball, I was able to meet a lot of people.My network widened and I was able to get more business prospects.)

Basketball in the Philippines is often used to earn goodwill from other people they might benefit from. Thus, basketball is a venue for bolstering social networks because it welcomes athletes to display their talents and skills, which will help them attract more interest and respect from their audience and potential supporters. Given all these, it is evident that many Filipinos see basketball as a platform to cultivate social relations that they believe to be a crucial step to advance in the socioeconomic ladder.

Indeed, it is typical for Filipino basketball enthusiasts to deliberately engage with basketball as much as the sport reinforces a strong personal affect, which then impacts their hopes for upward social mobility. The advantageous aspect that basketball elicits through personal connections exemplifies how feelings and emotions attributed to the sport, as carried out by social agents such as family and peers, greatly influence a person's motives for engaging in basketball. Most participants said that the media significantly influenced them growing up as it made them immitate their role models, hoping they, too, could be like their idols. Additionally, engaging in basketball contributes to one's upward social mobility through social connections and better economic opportunities. In a nutshell, basketball's perceived personal, economic, and social benefits revealed how deeply internalized basketball is among Filipino basketball enthusiasts.

Hybridizing Contemporary Philippine Basketball

Data indicated that Philippine basketball culture is hybrid in character. Given the enduring influence of American basketball, Philippine basketball culture is considerably honed when ascribed to particular Filipino values, ideas, and narratives in the sport. Moreover, the current demands of Filipino enthusiasts in terms of basketball practice in the Philippines demonstrate the need to create better systems, strategies, and mechanisms to bolster not just basketball but also other sports that are crucial in building the Filipino sports cultural identity.

As discussed, the American basketball culture heavily influences the Philippine basketball scene, but it is essential not to overlook the local ideational contributions in shaping Philippine basketball culture. Understanding Filipinos' role in the sport helps reveal the foundations of Philippine basketball. Data from interviews showed that the Filipinos' local ideational concepts, coupled with their practical demands for the development and practice of the sport, further hybridize the present Philippine basketball culture. Thus, understanding the Filipinos' contributions to the practice of the sport helps unpack the ideational foundations that reinforce Philippine basketball.

Most, if not all, the interviewees reiterated how Philippine basketball culture is substantially rooted in the concept of *puso,* which means heart. For Filipino basketball practitioners and other avid enthusiasts, *puso* captures a meaningful and creative expression that can be broadly understood as "lumalaban hanggang sa huling tibok," which means "fighting with all your might up until the last beat of your heart." It evokes the Filipinos' resilience and struggles—their unwavering fighting spirit— to give their all even in adverse game situations that seem unfavorable to the Filipinos' side. For many Filipino basketball enthusiasts, what *puso* means off the court encapsulates the symbolic struggles that Filipinos encounter in their everyday lives, epitomized by the saying "Basta may tiyaga, may nilaga," which roughly translates to "if one perseveres enough, success simply follows." (Divinagracia, 2020).

Undeniably, the essentiality of puso in Philippine basketball is manifested, particularly in international competitions where Filipinos display their talent on the world stage. The emotional tug of this *puso* battle cry, which has since been used post-2013, indicates not only the hunger for validation and redemption for the Filipinos to prove their mettle and excellence on the world stage but also a form of an assertive statement that the Philippines can also be a force to be reckoned with in basketball and not to be simply boxed and solely defined as the nation in Asia known for their "hoops and NBA craze" with no merits to prove its value. Hence, it is more than just a Filipino value that holds high regard in giving one's heart and soul in challenging times. *Puso* becomes a distinct national symbol that explicitly represents the Filipino national narratives of resilience, pride, and resolve. These national narratives, as a reiteration of the past and immortalized and mythicized in the present, epitomize the Filipinos' history of contesting dominant powers that have long overshadowed their sense of identity, as well as the everyday struggle that comes with internalizing the sense of inferiority that comes with the many years of subordination.

Another Filipino value that has become more than a source of national pride in Filipinos' engagement in basketball is the *bayanihan* spirit, which underscores a more profound sense of camaraderie across various Filipino communities. *Bayanihan* embodies the spirit of communal unity and cooperation (Guerrero & Sizoo, 2010). In basketball, *bayanihan* serves as a cultural bridge that brings individuals from various backgrounds together to enjoy basketball—transcending social and economic boundaries and reinforcing a united community. Additionally, many participants have turned to basketball for a sense of belongingness and unity among other enthusiasts because playing basketball allows one to express emotions and vent them through playing. The notion of unity and belonging in a community also creates a welcoming atmosphere where everyone is recognized as an integral part of the basketball community. The participants indicated that basketball has definitely increased and strengthened their social skills. Beyond reinforcing the Filipino community's sense of camaraderie and unity, utilizing the sense of togetherness on the court is also essential beyond interpersonal relationships. It has also become a strategic advantage as it fosters a positive and cohesive community dynamic that motivates enthusiasts to champion their advocacies through basketball.

Through the lens of Bhaba's cultural hybridity, the Filipino ideas, values, and narratives associated with *puso* and *bayanihan*, combined with the "new knowledge" that they have gained from American basketball culture, hone the practice of basketball in the Philippines and thereby constitutes its hybridization. More importantly, such fusion of the "new knowledge" from the American basketball culture and local ideational ascriptions on basketball make it an avenue for negotiating the Filipinos' sporting cultural identity—one that is reinforced and influenced by the United States yet also tries to resist such influence with local ideas and values. Ultimately, this realization is a manifestation of the ambivalence that happens in the Third Space, where Filipinos negotiate the aspects of their sporting culture from the components of basketball culture coming from the (formerly) colonial power that remains influential today and among themselves, as the (formerly) colonized Other and remains at a disadvantaged position.

It is crucial to understand that while Filipinos aim to reinforce their own unique basketball culture, there remains an insurmountable set of barriers that hamper the continued progress of the sport. Knowing fully well that despite incorporating Filipino elements in the sport, whether ideational or tactical, the reality remains that much has to be done to bridge the gaps between the Philippine basketball culture and that of the Americans. It is, therefore, imperative to make the sport able to adapt to styles that would suit better among the Filipinos and have more effective sports governance. These efforts, in turn, will also help them understand how basketball has been a significant driving force in bolstering the Philippine basketball culture.

The Filipino basketball community conveyed specific demands to address how the American basketball culture might have inadvertently contributed to hindering the development of Philippine basketball. Many Filipino basketball enthusiasts call for adequate resources as the lack thereof has hindered the progress of basketball in the Philippines. There are ideational aspects and practical demands that essentially put forward the Filipinoness of basketball, yet on the other hand, there is still a lingering reverence for the American way of doing basketball. There is also a strong clamor in the Philippine basketball community to invest more in innovative training methods and coaching styles and adopt the international style of the game other than the American style, as many better gaming styles would fit better Filipinos. For example, the faster, dynamic movement of play implemented in Europe would fit better for the physical stature of Filipino players. In this manner, the Filipinos will still be able to satisfy their preference for the individually spectacular action of the American style while also ensuring success by adopting the European system that suits the Filipinos' physical limitations. In other words, Filipinos call to "modernize" Philippine basketball by adopting Western standards and keeping pace with the innovations being employed elsewhere in the globe.

Although the Philippines is dubbed as one of the world's best basketball meccas, most facilities and equipment are substandard, especially in far-flung cities and rural zones. Many participants in this study shared that there has been minimal initiative in advancing Philippine basketball to provide all the necessary needs vital to the athletes' performance. Even across the regions in the Philippines, there is a significant disparity in the resources and facilities available, especially between the provinces and those in Metro Manila. There is also a lack of resources and insufficient funds to support other sports in the Philippines, such as football and badminton, especially for individual sports like track and field and gymnastics. Most participants in this study would concur that basketball has occupied the sole spotlight for viewership, media exposure, and institutional support at the expense of other sports that Filipinos have been known to excel at, like volleyball and football, and individual sports like gymnastics, boxing, the athletics, and weightlifting. Apart from the lack of support for other sports, another issue raised by the participants is the blatant inequality within the sport, most notably the significant gap and unequal distribution of government and institutional support towards women's basketball. Participants in this study generally pressed for a better representation of women in the sport as they believe that the status quo puts the limelight more towards men's basketball. This clamor for reform emphasizes that in the quest to boost the Filipinos' basketball culture, there must be adequate efforts to bridge gaps in the sports system that hinder the progress and development of Filipino basketball players and teams.

Although there is an overarching influence of American basketball, Philippine basketball culture is also significantly honed by ascribing particular Filipino values, ideas, and narratives in the practice of the sport, such as putting *puso* or infusing a *bayanihan* spirit in the conduct of the sport. This uncovers the fact that although American basketball has a significant hegemonic influence in the Philippines, the fusion of local ideational concepts and technical aspects in the sport illustrates both the subversion and reinforcement of the colonial and itself as the colonized Other.

Moreover, the current demands of Filipino enthusiasts in terms of basketball practice in the Philippines highlight the need for concrete changes in terms of institutional support and strategic overhaul to reinforce the contemporary practice of Philippine basketball. With all these, however, there is a striking presence of ambivalence in the current practice of the sport in the Philippines. On the one hand, there are ideational aspects and practical demands that essentially put forward the Filipinoness of basketball, yet on the other hand; there is still a lingering reverence for the American way of doing basketball.

Conclusions and Recommendations

The constant pitfalls and contentions hounding Philippine basketball can be better understood by analyzing the factors, reasons, and processes that perpetuate, internalize, and hybridize American basketball among Filipinos. Data showed that certain discourses play pivotal roles in maintaining the influence of the American basketball culture: American exceptionalism, capitalism, and exclusivist rhetoric. The study revealed why Filipino basketball enthusiasts continue accepting American basketball culture. Data indicated that Filipino basketball enthusiasts have internalized such a culture, especially since the sport elicits a strong personal affect and the allure of upward social mobility. Finally, the study probed the processes or the combination of ideational elements and practical demands that further hybridize Philippine basketball culture. The study revealed that the prevailing basketball culture influenced by the Americans is enriched with Filipino ideas, values, and narratives and the Filipino basketball enthusiasts' call for practical reforms in the country's basketball system.

Given the points above, this study concluded that the intermingling of the American and Philippine basketball cultures creates a hybrid basketball culture that is ambivalent at its core. On the one hand, such ambivalence is characterized by the Filipino enthusiasts' appeal and reverential regard for American basketball while subtly detesting such attraction to the former. On the other hand, they expressed the desire to empower and reinforce local Filipino strategies, techniques, and other ideational concepts in basketball while at the same time deprecating the perceived inadequacy and inferiority of traditional approaches in Philippine basketball. Future studies can narrow their analyses to the specific elements of American and Philippine basketball cultures. Future research can also delimit participants with hyphenated identities, like Filipino-Americans, as they best exemplify the straddling of two cultures and better unpack the complex dynamics in negotiating their identities, especially in diasporic settings. Future research can similarly touch upon the esports community to better understand the different societal and cultural processes within the new sporting frontiers. Ultimately, Philippine sporting agencies and institutions are encouraged to democratize the resources and media traction usually allotted for men's basketball towards the women's division and other sports to address the problems and controversies within the Philippine sporting landscape.

Acknowledgement

We would like to express gratitude to our thesis mentor, Ms. Krizza Janica B. Mahinay, MA, for her guidance, incisive comments, and comprehensive suggestions about our study. We also thank our adviser, Mr. John Harvey D. Gamas, MA, for his intelligent insights and wisdom. We deeply appreciate their unceasing patience, kindness, and enlightening guidance all throughout the research process. We would also like to thank our panelists, Ms. Monica A. Villa Abrille, MAS, Mr. Mansoor L. Limba, PhD, and Ms. Maria Lourdes S. Braceros, MSc, for their astute scrutiny of our study and their utmost generosity in sharing their respective areas of interest.

References

Aiello, T. (2022). *Hoops: A cultural history of basketball in America*. Rowman & Littlefield.

Antolihao, L. (2015). *Playing with the big boys: Basketball, American imperialism, and subaltern discourse in the Philippines*. University of Nebraska Press.

Aquino, K. (2015). More than a game: Embodied everyday anti-racism among young Filipino-Australian street ballers. *Journal of Intercultural Studies, 36*(2), 166–183. https://doi.org/10.1080/07256868.2015.100843

Bairner, A. (2003). Sport, nationality and postcolonialism in Ireland. In J. Bale

& M. Cronin (Eds.), *Sport and postcolonialism* (pp. 159-174). Routledge.

Bale, J. & Cronin, M. (Eds.). (2003). *Sport and postcolonialism.* Routledge.

Berri, D.J., Brook, S.L., Frick, B., Fenn, A.J., & Vicente-Mayoral, R. (2005). The short supply of tall people: Competitive imbalance and the National Basketball Association. *Journal of Economic Issues, 39*(4), (pp. 1029-1041),

Buras, B.V. (2002). *Sport and the changing definition of whiteness* [Master's thesis, Louisiana State University]. LSU DigitalCommons.

Cleophas, F.J. (Ed.) (2021). *Critical reflections on physical culture at the edges of empire.* African Sun Media. https://doi.org/10.2307/j.ctv1nzg1zm

Cleophas, F. (2021). *How colonial history shaped bodies and sport at the edges of empire.* The Conversation. https://theconversation.com/how-colonial-history-shaped-bodies-and-sport-at-the-edges-of-empire-166192

Delaney, T. (2015). The functionalist perspective on sport. In R. Giulianotti (Ed.), *Routledge handbook of the sociology of sport* (pp. 18-28). Routledge.

Divinagracia, A.A.G. (2020). *Philippine basketball, economy and politics: How the covid-19 pandemic hit the Filipinos' most beloved sport* [Conference session]. The Kyoto Conference on Arts, Media & Culture 2020, Kyoto, Japan. https://doi.org/10.22492/issn.2436-0503.2021.8

Eyles, A., Major, L.E., & Machin, S. (2022). Social mobility: past, present and future. *The Sutton Trust.*

Fuertes, R. J., (2024). *Andy Gemao only Filipino in NBA BWB Global Camp.* Inquirer.Net. https://sports.inquirer.net/553067/andy-gemao-only-fili-pino-in-nba-bwb-global-camp

Funk, D., Alexandris, K., & McDonald, H. (2008). *Consumer behavior in sport and events.* Routledge. https://doi.org/10.4324/9780080942858

Ganglani, N. (2022). *The price tag of winning a basketball championship.* Rappler. https://www.rappler.com/sports/uaap/basketball-philip-pines-price-tag-winning-varsity-championship/

Gems, G.R. (2016). *Sport and the American occupation of the Philippines: Rats, balls, and bayonets.* Lexington Books.

Gems, G. & Pfister, G. (2022). From imperialism to globalization: The transfer of sport forms. *Asian Journal of Sport History & Culture, 1*(1), 1-20. https://doi.org/10.1080/27690148.2022.2064716

Giulianotti, R. (2015). Sport and globalization. In R. Giulianotti (Ed.), *Routledge handbook of the sociology of sport,* (pp. 440-452). Routledge.Guerrero, S. H., & Sizoo, E. (2010). Filipino notions of responsibility: the shared identity of the self and the other. Responsibility and cultures of the world: Dialogue around a collective challenge, (20), 167.

Horton, P. (2011). Sport in Asia: Globalization, glocalization, asianization. In P. Pachura (Ed.), *New knowledge in a new era of globalization* (pp. 119-145). Intechopen. https://doi.org/10.5772/982

Huebner, S. (2013). Muscular christianity and the Western civilizing mission: Elwood S. Brown, the YMCA, and the idea of the Far Eastern Championship Games. *Diplomatic History, 39*(3), 532–557. https://doi.org/10.1093/dh/dht126

Huffman, T. (2023). *How USA basketball should change how they develop American basketball talent and why the NBA should change their style of play.* SportsRaid. https://medium.com/sportsraid/usa-basketball-should-change-how-they-develop-american-basketball-talent-and-why-the-nba-should-c8cac5e1ab70

Koklu, Y., Alemdaroglu, U., Kocak, F. U., Erol, A. E., & Findikoglu, G. (2011). Comparison of chosen physical fitness characteristics of Turkish professional players by division and playing position. *Journal of Human Kinetics, 30.* 99-106.

Leongson, R. (2022). *Curious on how much Filipino imports in Korea league make?* Spin.Ph. https://www.spin.ph/basketball/salaries-of-filipino-players-in-korea-basketball-league-a2437-20221103

Mambrol, N. (2017). *Ambivalence in post-colonialism.* Literary Theory and Criticism. https://literariness.org/2017/09/27/ambivalence-in-post-colonialism/

Mignolo, W. (2009). Epistemic disobedience, independent thought and de-colonial freedom. *Theory, Culture & Society 26* (7-8). https://doi.org/10.1177%2F0263276409349275

Mills, J. & Dimeo, P. (2003). When gold is fired it shines: Sport, the imagination and the body in colonial and postcolonial India. In J. Bale & M. Cronin (Eds.), *Sport and postcolonialism* (pp. 107-122). Routledge. https://doi.org/10.4324/9781003086772

Sallet P., Perrier, D., Ferret, J. M., Vitelli, V., & Baverel, G. (2005). Physiological differences in professional basketball players as a function of playing position and level of play. *The Journal of Sports Medicine and Physical Fitness, 45(3)*, 291-294

Sosis, R. & Kiper, J. (2022). Sport as a meaning-making system: Insights from the study of religion. *Religions, 13*(10). https://doi.org/10.3390/rel13100915

Vamplew, W. (2019). The commodification of sport: Exploring the nature of the sports product. *The International Journal of the History of Sport.* https://doi.org/10.1080/09523367.2018.1481832

Watson, D., Clark, L. A., McIntyre, C. W., & Hamaker, S. (1992). Affect, personality, and social activity. *Journal of personality and social psychology, 63*(6)

Widjaya, I. (2024). *The business of sports: NBA as a case study.* Noobpreneur. https://www.noobpreneur.com/2024/02/02/the-business-of-sports-nba-as-a-case-study/

Chapter 3

A Decolonial Study on the Sub-Regional Trade Integration of the BIMP-EAGA, 1994-2019

Olmer Gabriel S. Dagala, Pola Gabrielle E. Cuadrillero,
Monick D. Kimamao, Chetwin L. Señas,
& Alliyah Joy M. Yap

ABSTRACT

The examination of the BIMP-EAGA through a decolonial lens exposes unexplored factors that substantially affect the outcomes of sub-regional economic integration. Despite acknowledging the incompatibility of the Western model of integration in non-Western context, existing studies fell short in pointing out how exactly this model creates problems. To bridge such a gap, this decolonial study focused on analyzing BIMP-EAGA's sub-regional trade policies and paradigms, exposing the colonial legacies that marginalize traditional trade practices that obstruct their integration. Quijano's Colonial Matrix of Power theory was used to delink the colonial imprints within the three spheres of the BIMP-EAGA. In the sphere of authority, the supervision of policy elites resulted in statist strategies that imposed stringent controls on the movements of people and goods in the sub-region. In the sphere of economy, the governments, and SMEs of the BIMP-EAGA and MNCs have monopolized the resources and opportunities to profit from the region. In the sphere of knowledge and subjectivity, the policymaking elites have prioritized adherence to global standards and technological enhancement of the sub-region's trading practices. The study revealed that the BIMP-EAGA's trading policies and paradigms exemplify coloniality and raise issues relevant to the prioritization of territorial integrity, prohibition of traditional trade practices, and the privileging of SMEs and MNCs. All these colonial imprints have jeopardized the overall sub-regional integration.

Keywords: *BIMP-EAGA, Coloniality, Colonial Matrix of Power, Decolonial, Economic Integration*

Introduction

Existing academic literature indicates that economic integration and cooperation represent two distinct processes. Economic cooperation encompasses governmental involvement in commerce, stemming from agreements between multiple governments to regulate trade between participating national governments (Jeppie,

1987). Additionally, it is about "reducing" discrimination, allowing businesses equitable trade and impartial treatment (Kawai, 2004, p. 7). Meanwhile, economic integration involves a more extensive merging of economies, often requiring relinquishing a part of national sovereignty to create a more unified and efficient economic bloc (Krugman & Obstfel, 2003). Studies also indicated that there are statist and liberalist perspectives on how actors facilitate economic integration. Statists prioritize the state's control over economic activities and focus on safeguarding its economy and political authority over individual and civil society actions (Veg, 2019; Flores-Macías, 2010). Meanwhile, liberals oppose government policies that involve heavy state interventions, believing that such interventions can stifle open competition and free trade, hindering the development of peaceful relations (Dorn, 2007).

Furthermore, studies have shown that economic integration has early and modern forms. The pre-modern means and modes of economic integration focused on non-Western contexts. Historical records indicate that non-Western regions have long-standing regional relationships predating the coining of the term "integration" and the practice of economic integration among European nations (Manggala, 2013). Modern modes of integration encompass formal and informal forms that shape and guide various initiatives' economic trajectories and dynamics. One of these forms is the *de jure* or the formal arrangement. This approach strictly adheres to institutionalized policies and agreements among member states, providing a stable framework for trade cooperation and reducing economic disparities among member states (Hiratsuka & Kimura, 2008; Bensassi et al., 2019). In contrast, the *de facto* or informal arrangement follows a more flexible and adaptable approach, catering to diverse interests and addressing issues within the cooperation. This setup allows for more fluid and responsive engagement within the economic integration, promoting stable and efficient trade cooperation and the ability to mitigate economic disparities among member states (Hiratsuka & Kimura, 2008; Besassi et al., 2019).

Modern forms of economic integration have Eurocentric

bias. The development of this bias started in the late 18th and 19th centuries when colonial powers intensified their control over territories, implementing assertive and exclusionary governance methods (Rana, 2012). In the said period, Western imperial forces in Asia established clear boundaries and imposed direct or indirect control over trade, customs, and access to inland waterways. Additionally, European integrations have emerged, driven by a modern standard imposed by European powers, where non-European institutions failing to align with European standards were considered unsuccessful (Baumann, 2021). Eurocentrism is also facilitated by globalization as it fosters continuous global expansion and market liberalization, demanding increased access, economic freedom, and deregulation (Diamond, 2019, p. 91). There is the "great globalization disruption," which causes integration of labor, capital, markets, and technological and economic transformation and, at the same time, triggers more rigorous national protectionist measures to shield individuals from market pressures that may undermine established ideological agreements and alliances (Diamond, 2019, p. 12). However, existing literature does not extensively discuss how the Western-influenced structure of economic integration itself, employed by its participants, can influence the economic integration's successes and/or failure.

An example of a modern economic integration is the Brunei Darussalam-Indonesia-Malaysia-Philippines East ASEAN Growth Area (BIMP-EAGA). This sub-regional integration exemplifies the profound influence of Western development ideologies in Southeast Asia (Chia, 2013). Established due to ASEAN's shortcomings in addressing regional development disparities, BIMP-EAGA adopted a Western-modeled approach to regionalism, emphasizing openness, inclusion, and outward-looking development (Aung-Thwin, 2014; BIMP-EAGA, 2006). This focus on accessibility and mobility aligns with Western development standards (Turner & Kühn, 2019). Notably, BIMP-EAGA's subsequent development plans, including the Roadmap Development Plan (RDP) 2006-2010, Implementation Blueprint (IB) 2012-2016, and BIMP-EAGA

Vision (BEV) 2025, all adhere to Western standards, particularly the customs, immigration, quarantine, and security (CIQS) protocols (Asian Development Bank, 2006). While the CIQS protocol facilitates cross-border movement, it also disrupts traditional trade practices within the EAGA, potentially hindering full economic integration among the member-states (Bayley, 2016). In this regard, this study "decolonized" the long-established Western paradigms and policy recommendations shaping BIMP-EAGA by analyzing the colonial influences of its integration efforts. This study went back to the sub-region's pre-modern trade practices and identified how colonial legacies are embedded in the paradigms and policies of the BIMP-EAGA which paradoxically obstruct the sub-regional integration.

This study utilized Anibal Quijano's "Coloniality of Power" to analyze colonial influences in BIMP-EAGA's maritime policies and paradigm. This theory explains the hegemony, power, and control system of colonialism through the narratives of the three essential concepts: *coloniality*, *modernity*, and *rationality* (Quijano & Ennis, 2000 as cited in Mignolo, 2007b). *Coloniality* is a pattern of dominance that originates from an unseen portion of history (Mignolo, 2007a). It is a basis of the power structure that codified the racial/ethnic categorization of human beings manifested in all aspects of life and spheres of society (Quijano, 2000, p. 342). *Coloniality* underscores how policies, institutions, and organizations adhere to laws established by a system rooted in colonial standards. Moreover, *coloniality* is manifested in three spheres called the Colonial Matrix of Power collectively: the *sphere of authority*, the *sphere of economy*, and the *sphere of knowledge* and *subjectivity*. Firstly, the *sphere of authority* pertains to the elites' governance regulation and establishment of territorial boundaries by the nation-state. In the BIMP-EAGA, member states have adopted a strict statist approach to policy making. Secondly, the *sphere of economy* elaborates on the capitalization and monopolization of goods and services. Within this sphere, it is observed that the member states of BIMP-EAGA enable MNCs and SMEs to influence policy-making decisions. Thirdly, the *sphere of knowledge* exhibits Western cognitive processes, where BIMP-EAGA's policymaker elites rationalized that development should be grounded in Western globalization methods and trends.

The next concept is *modernity*. This concept refers to the ways in which social activity or structure arose in Europe. *Modernity* is an orientation towards the future determined by Western expectations, reshaping the present circumstances of indigenous lives and deeming them of lesser value (Quijano & Ennis, 2000). *Rationality*, the third concept, pertains to the domination of the Western perspective in producing knowledge and views (Quijano, 2000). *Rationality* is evident in the established Western thinking in the conceptualization of institutions and in maritime laws and trade policies, which have silenced and suppressed the histories, subjects, and knowledge of indigenous maritime trading practices. *Modernity* and *rationality* are combined to understand and identify the *coloniality* embedded within the system and the knowledge production of BIMP-EAGA's maritime connectivity and trading policies and paradigms. These three concepts illustrate that Western imprint in the integration impedes traditional maritime practices, prompting the need to produce decolonized maritime policies. Hence, Quijano suggests delinking *modernity* and *rationality* from *coloniality* (Mignolo, 2007b). Utilizing the delinking process causes a decolonial shift, bringing different epistemologies, principles of knowing and understanding, and, as a result, other economies, politics, and ethics. The delinking process is called Decolonialism, which reveals the colonial patterns of knowledge production and power play between the former colonizer and the previously colonized (De Lissovoy & Bailón, 2019). The decolonial lens of Quijano's Coloniality of Power then uncovers and delinks the colonial underpinnings of nation-states among the BIMP-EAGA member-states from the domination of *coloniality* in adopting territorial sovereignty and policy formulation concerning economic integration.

This research is a qualitative case study and used thematic analysis to process data. Researchers utilized the year 1994 as the starting point for the analyses, as it was the year when the BIMP-EAGA was established. In the following years, primary sources like the Memorandum of Understandings (MOUs) were made until the 1997 Asian Financial Crisis—a crisis that halted economic activities in the region and the BIMP-EAGA. These MOUs are the Memorandum of Understanding on Transit and Inter-State Transport of Goods and the Memorandum of Understanding on Establishing and Promoting Efficient and Integrated Sea Linkages. When the region bounced back, BIMP-EAGA produced the Roadmap Development Plan of 2006-2010, the Implementation Blueprint 2012-2016, and the BIMP-EAGA Vision 2025. Additionally, other primary sources were key informant interviews (KII), identified through purposive and snowball sampling. These KIIs are the Mindanao Development Authority (MinDA), Palawan Council for Sustainable Development (PCSD), as well as the Consulate Generals of Malaysia and the Republic of Indonesia in Davao City. However, due to the strict information control and confidentiality of the Brunei Embassy and the unresponsiveness of the country's BIMP-EAGA representative offices, researchers were not able to conduct interviews in relation to Brunei. Nevertheless, primary sources also encompassed materials sourced from official government websites, particularly in the case of Brunei Darussalam, to compensate for the lack of interview data. Meanwhile, the secondary sources were extracted from published materials by experts on the pre-modern activities of pre-modern members of BIMP-EAGA. Lastly, the researchers limited the timeframe of the study until the year 2019 due to the COVID-19 pandemic, which caused delays in the initiatives within the sub-regional organization.

Premodern Trading Practices in East Maritime Southeast Asia

Premodern maritime trading in East Maritime Southeast Asia revolved around three key elements: network-based strategy, cosmic-based ruling, and the transformative influence of Islamicization. Firstly, the network-based strategy involved diplomatic marriages, trade network establishment, and raiding alliances, which helped rulers maintain control and stabilize influence (Abinales & Amoroso, 2017; Warren, 2007). Secondly, the cosmic-based ruling was rooted in local cosmological beliefs, legitimizing rulers' authority and shaping political frameworks (Traube, 1986; Manggala, 2013; Arhem, 2016). Thirdly, Islamicization further solidified alliances, leading to the emergence of trading ports and facilitating trade networks (Najtama, 2018; Latiff and Hassan, 2009; Mostert, 2018). These traditional components significantly influenced the selection and empowerment of rulers in maritime trading chiefdoms. Marriage alliances were crucial for forming trade networks and alliances, while raiding alliances served as economic and political tools (Junker, 1999; Robequain, 1969). Cosmic-based ruling structures centered on rulers' divine authority, maintaining balance, and regulating goods within chiefdoms (Wolters, 1999; Healey, 1985). Islamicization played a pivotal role in fostering trade activities and networks, facilitating alliances, and accelerating interactions among peoples in the region (Majul, 1966). This historical trajectory underscores the complex interplay of factors that aided maritime trading activities in the sub-region, shaping its economic and political landscape.

Moreover, mercantile practices formed the backbone of pre-colonial maritime trading networks in the sultanates of Brunei, Ternate, Makassar, Maguindanao, and Sulu. Such practices facilitated the acquisition, circulation, and exchange of various goods. Barter trading was prevalent, allowing for the exchange of goods and dissemination of technologies, beliefs, and cultural practices (Smith, 1999; Hall, 1985; Warren, 2002; Abinales & Amoroso, 2014; Borschberg, 2020). Other trading practices were engaged by different groups like highland hunters, lowland cultivators, and coastal communities (Hall, 1985; Winzeler et al., 1976). The acquisition of high-value commodities like camphor, pepper, and sea cucumbers played a pivotal role in regional trade, fostering alliances and network expansion (Chang & Tagliacozzo, 2011; Warren, 2008; Andaya, 2002; Sutherland, 2021). Slave raiding, integral to manpower acquisition, shaped the labor force and economic dynamics of the region. In these times, slaves were utilized in various capacities and even integrated into local communities over time (Cotterell, 2014; Robequain & Laborde, 1969; Reid, 1983; Laarhoven, 1986). These practices were crucial for sustaining the political and economic influence of the sultanates, supporting their military expansion and trade endeavors (Warren, 1987; Reid, 1990; Reid, 2017). Despite variations, such practices contributed significantly to the thriving maritime trade in East Maritime Southeast Asia.

The sultanates also fostered vibrant maritime trade with neighboring empires. This network is characterized by minimal restrictions and robust diplomatic ties facilitated by dispatching envoys (Warren, 1981; Nicholl, 1983; Healey, 1985; Warren, 2007). This set-up was aided by adopting Malay as a common language among the sultanates, which was crucial in promoting seamless trade and cultural exchange. Malay was a vital bridge between trade and diplomacy in diverse cultures (Sutherland, 2003; Cotterell, 2014; Lopez, 2014). Variants like Low Malay and High Malay adapted to different social classes and trade situations, like foreign merchants, who relied on proficient locals to navigate the intricate trading landscapes of the sultanates (Bausani, 1960; Rafferty, 1984; Adelaar, 2000). As exemplified by the sultanates of Brunei and Sulu's diplomatic ties with China, the dispatching of envoys played a pivotal part as well, as it allowed rulers to consolidate power and expand trade networks (Gamas, 2020, p. 21; Healey, 1985; Hayase, 2007; Warren, 1981; Hutterer, 1977; Hopkins, 1912). Trade routes also served as an important conduit for commerce, where the strategic ports of Makassar, Brunei, and Jolo facilitated trade between East and West Asia (Morstet, 2018). Lastly, river routes nurtured trade activities and fostered alliances within the sultanates of Maguindanao and Butuan (Gamas, 2020, p. 23; Hall, 1985; Hayase, 2007; Kian, 2013; Abinales & Amoroso, 2017). All these factors collectively depict a scenario where the absence of a Westphalian system within the network allowed the sultanates to facilitate a smooth and flourishing flow of goods and people.

With this historical backdrop, we can evidently picture the maritime trade practices in East Maritime Southeast Asia from the 12th to 17th century that preceded the modern system in the BIMP-EAGA sub-region. These trade practices evolved to accommodate growing trade activities. Alliances formed through marriage and raiding, mandalic power structures, and Islamic beliefs legitimized trade expansion and political ties. Unique mercantile practices like barter trading, exchanging high-valued goods, and acquiring manpower facilitated maritime trade within regional entrepots. Trade routes, the employment of the Malay language in trading activities, and the dispatch of tributary envoys furthered trade access and privileges, responding effectively to international trade demands. These practices laid the foundation for a robust maritime trade in the sub-region, contrasting the Westphalian constraints examined in the subsequent chapters.

Coloniality in BIMP-EAGA's Trading Paradigms and Policies

The Colonial Matrix of Power encompasses the *spheres of knowledge* and *subjectivity, authority*, and *economy*. The first sphere, *knowledge and subjectivity*, show control in producing and disseminating knowledge and beliefs that sustain colonial dominance (Quijano & Ennis, 2002). The domination of Western-centric perspectives shapes the rationalization process and permeates the individuals' erceptions within BIMP-EAGA. Policymaker elites prioritize economic development through a globalized modernization influenced by Western ideals and leveraging technological advancements to bolster ICT capacities. This modernization drive is evident in creating ICT policies to foster the economic growth of BIMP-EAGA.

Policymakers in the sub-region believe that this heavy inclination to technology-based mechanisms aids the knowledge of the task forces on the cross-border activities of individuals. ICT speedily allows the authorities to identify the "illegal" practices of individuals subject to policing actions. As stated in the Implementation Blueprint 2016-2020, digitization policies are perceived as vehicles for formalizing and streamlining the safer movement of goods, services, and people. Ultimately, these policies are targeted to contribute to economic prosperity in the sub-region. Moreover, policymakers rationalize ICT as a strategy that aids the modernization of transport and trade facilitation within the sub-region. Such rationalization of ICT entails having online systems for the efficient exchange of information in monitoring the entry and exit of people and goods within the sub-region (BIMP-EAGA, 2012). This mode is believed to help maintain security (BIMP-EAGA, 2012). Additionally, this strategic plan identified definite mechanisms, such as the BIMP-EAGA Facilitation Center (BFC), which was responsible for providing technical assistance to project developers and implementers, and the BIMP-EAGA Business Council (BEBC) that controls private sector investments in the BIMP-EAGA projects.

Other initiatives of the BIMP-EAGA that align with Western models are reflected in their broader legalization efforts to regulate cross-border activities. Digitalization seeks to make coordination efficient within and beyond the subregion. This is in their MOU in Establishing and Promoting Efficient and Integrated Sea Linkages to smoothen the coordination of the inside and outside of the BIMP-EAGA (BIMP-EAGA, 2007). MinDA representative, Ms. Gilayo (personal communication, September 5, 2022) stated that economic integration is about stepping up in terms of digitalization and modernization by having online communication, data storage, as well as the procurement of machines for efficient CIQS enforcement. She added that machines could do the work, and there would be less human interaction in inspecting ships before they go to another island, so the movement of ships could be more efficient (Gilayo, personal communication, September 5, 2022). The plan indicates the significance of technological use in the sub-region in enhancing surveillance and control within the focus areas.

Aside from modernizing the physical instruments for economic development, the BIMP-EAGA policymakers thought of modernizing the educational competencies of individuals by promoting ICT knowledge and skills. This upgrade will produce a more skilled labor force in ICT. Policymakers invest in this modernization of education initiatives, just like Western countries, as they believe this could cultivate the exchange of information and foreign investment to help develop and enlarge local markets. BIMP-EAGA affirms that creating such ICT policies and plans intends to support trade development by improving the literacy rate in order to develop new products and services that connect people (BEV Connectivity Pillar - Information and Communication Technology. The Strategic Priority number 3 of the document indicates that professionals of the ICT sector within the BIMP-EAGA sub-region will have registration in a system that will identify each individual's educational and work capacity. The interview respondents all agreed on the idea of modernizing the education system. This plan aims to help attain and maintain the international standards of education needed to promote trade and interconnectivity within the sub-region.

There are specific examples in which policymakers of the member-states exhibit their rationalization of using technology for economic growth. The Malaysian Consulate, for example, raised that their hedge-based economy, or K-economy, is participated by the private sector that consists of collaboration aiming to shift from a traditional manufacturing-based economy to one that is generated by intellectual capital and technological advancements (Leave a Nest, 2023). Brunei also allowed Huawei to help the government nurture its citizens' ICT talents through its training programs to develop skills and bridge cultures through technological communication (Xinhua, 2022). EY Indonesia (2022) also indicates that digital transformation in the country has become the primary drive of economic growth, having a fit-to-purpose structure that facilitates collaboration between foreign companies and local partners. Lastly, in the Philippines, intelligent farming practices, facilitated by Internet of Things (IoT) sensors and data analytics, are conducted to optimize crop yields and enhance resource efficiency Espinosa (2023).

Policymakers' thinking process displays that the minds behind the sub-regional integration rationalized development plans that adhere to the perpetuation of colonial legacies. For this study, elites meant policymakers who craft these documents and plans have a fixed idea of how to view and create the conduct of *modernity*, believing that *modernity* is the critical answer to economic growth in the sub-region (Quijano & Ennis, 2000). The perspective of these policymakers on technology is based on the Western belief that technology is a crucial development driver. The colonial experiences introduced a new world order that significantly disrupted the cultural, structural, and societal norms of indigenous communities residing in the focal regions. Consequently, this historical context continues to profoundly impact contemporary discourse, contributing to the discrediting and marginalization of indigenous knowledge within the broader societal narrative. How the policymakers have perceived economic development as a prerequisite to reaching international standards indicates that the sub-region needs to become economically competitive and technologically savvy. However, while the people in the sub-region are open to more advanced technology, they also strongly desire to safeguard their traditional practices. The belief that new technologies are drivers of economic growth, in turn, can impose negative consequences on the people within the subregion and the integration of the BIMP-EAGA.

The *sphere of authority* is a concept that focuses on the political and institutional power of the elites (as cited in Mignolo, 2007b). Elites such as policymakers, MNCs, and SMEs hold power in the organization and control of political structures and governance. However, it is the policymakers who decide whether to involve the private sector. *Coloniality*, according to Quijano (2000), lies in the presence of unequal power dynamics established by the colonial powers and furthers the endurance of the colonizers' influence, colonialism, on contemporary systems of authority. In the BIMP-EAGA sub-region, Quijano's theory reveals that historical legacies and entrenched power structures wield significant influence over the prevailing *rationality*. The persistent presence of specific hierarchies and inequalities characterizes this *rationality*. *Coloniality* is unmistakably evident in the sub-region's practices, policies, and paradigms. BIMP-EAGA adopts a statist approach to territorial governance, with the elites exercising strict controls and advocating for policies that reflect their authority.

In the context of the BIMP-EAGA, policy decisions, and agreements are made mostly among government officials and the private sector, making them the elites that formulated, for example, the CIQS regulations and ICT mechanisms modernization plan of the economic integration (BIMP-EAGA, 2009; BIMP-EAGA, 2012; BIMP-EAGA, 2017). The policymaking process of the elites displays a statist top-down approach. For instance, policy sector conferences were conducted in the Policy Formulation Division of the MinDA to discuss and convey grassroots interests and realities to the national government (Gilayo, personal communication, September 5, 2022). Sector interests are then lobbied to become policy in the House of Representatives.

These adaptations of top-down approaches signify that the national capital is implementing these government acts, which are concrete evidence of *coloniality*. Williams (2008) echoes the significance of MNCs and SMEs utilizing BIMP-EAGA as an economic platform, emphasizing the benefits. He argues that Malacañang endeavors to nurture and endorse the economic network of BIMP-EAGA by unveiling a concealed political agenda that contradicts the aspirations of Philippine national economic integration ideals. MNCs and SMEs engage in 'rent-seeking' behaviors, pursuing government privileges to maintain a competitive edge. Given the substantial financial backing from entities offering Official Development Assistance (ODA), such as the Asian Development Bank (ADB), the Association of Southeast Asian Nations (ASEAN), and USAID's GEM Program for Mindanao's development and economic growth, the allure for politicians based in Manila and other established kin groups to engage in 'rent-seeking' becomes particularly compelling. These rent-seeking behaviors manifest through active participation in policymaking, ostensibly in support of economic integration, but with a primary focus on securing more significant advantages for MNCs and SMEs participating at the BIMP-EAGA. Consequently, these activities neglect the locals in the focus areas who would otherwise directly benefit from these initiatives.

Other coordinating offices of the BIMP-EAGA have official mandates wherein they exemplify top-down approach bureaucracies similar to the case of the Philippines. The Ministry for Economic Affairs has Indonesia's Presidential Regulation Number 37 of 2020. In Brunei, His Majesty is the Prime Minister, Minister of Defence, Minister of Finance and Economy, and Minister of Foreign Affairs. As the Sultan and Yang Di-Pertuan of Brunei Darussalam, His Majesty is also the Supreme Executive Authority in Brunei Darussalam. Lastly, the Ministry of Economy in Malaysia has the Ministerial Functions Act of 1969.

The BIMP-EAGA's coordinating offices can recommend and coordinate with the proper agencies on technical support and assistance. In the context of sub-regional integration, there is a discernible emphasis on prioritizing various sectors such as agriculture, industry, commerce, infrastructure, environment, and technology. These sectors often seek direct or indirect support from the national government and its designated agencies responsible for their implementation. Unlike the redistribution process of wealth within the Sultanates during the pre-modern times, the autonomy and authority to directly redistribute the wealth among people did not require an extensive bureaucratic process (Hayase, 2007). Premier local chiefs within local chiefdoms laid out the redistribution of wealth under the Sultan.

Meanwhile, in the ICT sector, the BIMP-EAGA conducts regular meetings involving the private sector, specifically the SMEs and the MNCs from each member state (BIMP-EAGA, 2017, p.50). The private sector has a "fifth country" status at the BIMP-EAGA business council, giving them an equal voice in Senior Officials' Meetings (BIMP-EAGA, 2017, p.50). These elites of the BIMP-EAGA, who collaborate with the government in crafting and implementing policies, highlighted further the need for a faster mode of transacting trade within the sub-region through ICT-led projects. Moreover, this kind of *rationality* is further manifested through the BEV's Connectivity Pillar - Information and Communication Technology (ICT) Sector Strategy and the BIMP-EAGA Roadmap to Development 2006-2010. These sectors indicate that the private sector is encouraged to participate in the trade industries, focusing on connectivity and cybersecurity and crafting the industries' mechanism operation (BIMP-EAGA, 2017, p. 29; BIMP-EAGA, 1995, p. 6).

Presently, the setup of BIMP-EAGA shows the collaboration between the private sector and state officials, allowing them to agree. In this regard, the MNCs and SMEs in the BIMP-EAGA member-states have the discretion of where and how to direct the project planning and implementation of the ICT sectors and clusters (BIMP-EAGA, 2017). This setup means that the MNCs and SMEs have also become the main actors in the decision-making processes of the modernization projects and initiatives to enhance the trading transactions, sidelining the people's perspectives and directly affecting their livelihood. The government, together with the MNCs and SMEs, are at the top of the hierarchy in the policy-making process of the BIMP-EAGA. This arrangement is distinct from pre-modern times. During such a period, there was no stringent top-down approach to allocating authority for legal decision-making processes, and the rapidity of the trading transactions did not dictate it (Warren, 2007). Trading in pre-modern times depended heavily on the unpredictable state of seas and rivers for the mobilization of goods and the availability of goods procured within hinterlands (Pye et al., 2009; Cotterell, 2014).

The researchers have identified examples of MNCs and SMEs in different focus areas. In the WBEC, the Malaysian state of Sabah has the Sawit Kinabalu Group company, which specializes in creating palm oil products. Its main activities are cultivating, processing, procuring, and trading fresh fruit bunches, crude palm oil, and palm kernels (BIMP-EAGA, 2017). In Brunei Darussalam, Simpor

Pharma Sdn. Bhd. is Brunei Darussalam's leading pharmaceutical and health supplement manufacturer and a major exporter of halal products (BIMP-EAGA, 2017). West Kalimantan has the Perkebunan Nusantara XIII (PTPN XIII), an agribusiness company with operations in East Kalimantan, South Kalimantan, and Central Kalimantan. Its operational activities cover palm oil and rubber cultivation, production, and trading (BIMP-EAGA, 2017). In the Philippine Island of Mindanao, the RD Corporation (RD) is a diversified Philippine business whose products cover agribusiness, deep sea fishing, shipbuilding and repair, manufacturing, seafood processing, financial services, and realty (BIMP-EAGA, 2017). In North Sulawesi, Indonesia, Plantation Dimembe Nyiur Agripro (DNA) is a desiccated coconut manufacturing company in North Minahasa. The company packs its desiccated coconut in multi-ply Kraft paper bags with inner sealed polylines and outer poly woven bags in packs. Lastly, in Sabah, Malaysia, Life Water Industries Sdn Bhd has branches in Lahad Datu and Kota Kinabalu, producing several quality beverages. Its leading product, K2 17 Stages Purified Drinking Water, is named for the 17 stages of the water purification system used to produce it.

The SMEs and the MNCs are among the policymaking elites that ground their *rationality* and perspectives of *modernity* based on the West's neo-liberal economic perspective. These elites significantly facilitate BIMP-EAGA's economic liberalization to create more economic opportunities in which these MNCs are gearing their strategies to abide by Western trading trends. However, it demonstrates that the policies are ineffective in creating equal income distribution and that only the SMEs and the MNCs benefit from the BIMP-EAGA platform. Consequently, the plans of BIMP-EAGA for policymaking procedures may lead to MNCs and SMEs wielding significant influence over the processes of shaping regulations to favor their interests, which is the manifestation of the Coloniality of Power.

Ideally, BIMP-EAGA's regulations and policies should benefit more undeveloped and less income-generating areas in the region (BIMP-EAGA, 2017). However, because of the design of the structures of authority, elites now are privileged to use the resources and labor of marginalized communities, thereby perpetuating disparities in power and influence within the region. This privileging of policy elites, or the government authorities, SMEs, and the MNCs over the marginalized communities in the focus areas mirrors historical patterns of colonialism where dominant powers apply their authority and economic interests on colonized regions, resulting in the subjugation of local populations. Additionally, the modernization of the CIQS trade facilitation system widens the gap among the member-states, which is influenced by the lingering colonial economic structures within the modernized trade facilitation system. This modernization poses a risk to the stability of economic integration. The modernization and standardization of trade facilitation protocols in the focus areas introduced an 'ideal model' for economic development based on Western ideals. However, this approach comes at the expense of marginalized communities and individuals engaged in traditional maritime trading.

Finally, the *sphere of economy* depicts monopolization in labor and capitalist enterprises (Quijano and Ennis, 2000). The government, SMEs, and MNCs monopolize resources such as commodities and services as part of the protocols and regulations for capitalization under their control. The sphere shows the colonial patterns in the economic development policies formulated by the elites, such as modernized CIQS protocols to regulate and oversee the movement of people and goods, ensuring compliance with international standards and enhancement of the ICT capacity of the sub-region. The central government, wielding authority to monopolize resource control within its jurisdiction through policymaking, facilitates heightened involvement of MNCs and SMEs in the subregion to meet its policies, albeit at the cost of the livelihoods of individuals residing in key focus areas within BIMP-EAGA.

BIMP-EAGA authorities who prioritize trade facilitation by improving the efficiency of CIQS and upgrading ICT infrastructure amplify the historical colonial dynamics within BIMP-EAGA. These elements of 'liberalized economy' in the guise of reinforcement of the Westphalian notion of protecting the state, which European colonial powers have been promoting, further silence the marginalized voices of the people affected in the focus areas and their livelihood (Quijano, A., & Ennis, M., 2000). These paradigms urge the imposition of paying trading taxes, duty taxes, certifications, and surveillance technology as part of the protocols. In the pre-modernization period, the maritime polity established and maintained their control over the maritime trading activities of East Maritime Southeast Asia, among other local chiefdoms, by imposing trading port fees on merchant ships (Warren, 2007). These trading port fees were utilized to control the trading activities of foreign merchants within the premodern polities but did not prevent the participation of local and foreign merchants. In the modern age, policies and practices of the colonial powers in the colonized regions reverberated through new structures and modern procedures that labeled the traditional trading practices as outdated forms of the new age of liberalized economy. Moreover, the members of traditional trade practices have been deemed "illegal" by the name of national law for not meeting international standards and procedures.

Implementing the CIQS removes trade barriers and zero-tariff trade between the parties to have a more unrestrained and safer movement of people and goods following the international minimum standards (Joseph, personal communications, 2022). However, the formalization and standardization of maritime regulations by the International Maritime Organization (IMO) have given rise to a predicament among local fisher folks and navigators. Mr. Romeo Montenegro, the Executive Director of MinDA explained that following IMO standards, wooden vessels are no longer permitted to navigate international waters (Doquila, 2019). This effectively prevents fishers who are using traditional boats from venturing further and engaging in cross border trade. The new institutionalized standards for maritime operations have stipulated that only steel-made ships can operate in international maritime domains. Although there is an attempt to minimize the effects of the standards and regulations of CIQS, there is still a monopoly over the movement of goods, people, and services, from which only the big companies can benefit. Centuries of fishing activities by the local fisher folks within the focus areas, which use traditional methods and ships, are disrupted and are now prohibited.

The introduction of Western standards and certifications even regulated the usage of the high-value commodity, the edible bird's nest. The Palawan Council for Sustainable Development (2017) put up Administrative Order no. 8a s. 2003 requires a permit and/or clearances for collecting, extracting, and removing edible bird's nests found within the caves in the province of Palawan in the Philippines. In the *Sphere of Economy*, this administrative order operates within a broader context influenced by the Coloniality of Power. Although the criteria serve as economic regulations for environmental protection, this idea reflects historic power imbalances that echo colonial-era practices that shaped access, legitimacy, and privilege in economic activities related to the extraction of edible bird's nests in the region. The idea is a colonial imprint because the government and the private sector limit the people who can legitimately harvest the said resources, such as those with the capacity and access to acquire government-issued permits to extract the edible bird's nest. The permitted actors would then have the power to capitalize on the resources. Such a statist approach discriminates against the indigenous local communities living in the focus areas.

According to the BIMP-EAGA Vision 2025 document, the economic integration of the geographically disjointed sub-region is one of the challenges that BIMP-EAGA faces. One of the perceived solutions to this problem is the implementation of Radio-Frequency Identification (RFID) technology (ADB, 2006, pg. 13). This technology is said to expedite and smoothen the way for the flow of goods and transportation within the sub-region by its highly advanced surveillance technology used to track stolen goods or even track people involved in kidnapping or other crimes. However, the surveillance plans of the BIMP-EAGA also manifest the intention to monopolize the flow of maritime trading activities of the sub-region, which prohibits the economies of member-states from integrating rather than promoting a more unrestrained movement of goods, people, and services through modernization trade facilitation. Ironically, this entails control over marginalized communities and their activities. These development plans displaced the indigenous populations and caused a gradual erosion of these communities' established systems of governance and authority. Policymakers prioritize macroeconomic development and the building of new advanced infrastructures at the expense of the maritime livelihoods of indigenous communities (Domínguez & Luoma, 2020).

The modernization of CIQS and the digitalization of ICT exacerbates the perpetuating colonial legacy of securitization of territorial boundaries. In contrast to these modern regulations, controlling the acquisition and flow of goods within premodern polities was a way to supply the demands of the burgeoning maritime trade and increase the ruler's political influence for effective leadership (Chang & Tagliacozzo, 2011). The control of the trading activities aimed not to have it monopolized by the concentrated power among the few elite entities but to ensure the seamless functionality of maritime trading activities within East Maritime Southeast Asia. The modernization and digitalization processes reflect and perpetuate the control of labor and capitalistic enterprise, a pattern of colonial power and domination.

To summarize, documents and informant responses revealed the deep and abiding influence of Western-centric vision in BIMP-EAGA's economic policies. This influence is evident in the *sphere of authority*, where elitist-driven statist strategies impose stringent controls, leading to the branding of traditional maritime practices as smuggling. In the *sphere of economy*, capitalist pursuits aim to liberalize trade markets and modernize CIQS and ICT resources, potentially exacerbating disparities and neglecting long-term sustainability. The *sphere of knowledge and subjectivity* reflects colonial standards, illegalizing traditional maritime trading activities and invalidating centuries-old trading links among member-states.

Coloniality in BIMP-EAGA: An Obstacle to Integration

The identified colonial patterns in the policies and initiatives within BIMP-EAGA reflect a strengthening of the Westphalian system of nation-states and the fact that Western modernization standards raise specific concerns. This emphasis produced territorial integrity issues that hindered economic integration within the region. Before the Westphalian system, Sultanates primarily traded without the concept of territorial borders. Their concerns revolved around colonial interference, not state boundaries (Manggala, 2013). This contrasted sharply with the current situation, where territorial disputes within the sub-region significantly impact maritime trade. BIMP-EAGA modernization and regulations regarding territorial integrity exacerbate the problems arising from disputed territories. For example, the Sabah dispute between Malaysia and the Philippines creates tension that hinders economic integration within BIMP-EAGA. CIQS and ICT mechanisms, designed to promote the freer movement of people and goods, have instead become tools to police the disputed area, restricting economic development in the sub-region. This dispute has been a major impediment to normal and stable relations between the Philippines and Malaysia for nearly three decades (Asreemoro, 2008). This was emphasized by *Joseph* of Palawan Council for Sustainable Development (personal communication, September 14, 2022), who noted that:

> The conflict of Sovereignty... one of the primary obstacles that we have, the Sultanate of Sulu and, vicariously, the Republic of the Philippines have a claim on Sabah. It trickles down. They affect trade relations and our initiatives. So, to the point where the Malaysian side, Kuala Lumpur, has informally put a hold on our plans to integrate a trading route from Manila to Palawan, Palawan to Kodat, and Kota Kinabalu to Indonesia.

Territorial issues cripple the attainment and completion of inter-state economic plans within BIMP-EAGA, which threaten the integration (*Joseph,* personal communication, September 14, 2022). These disputes create implacable barriers to integration, prioritizing perceived borders as a major obstacle. The contested nature of these borders and the associated protectionist measures further exacerbate tensions and restrict cross-border cooperation.

Moreover, the presence of the label "illegal" immigrants in the BIMP-EAGA sub-region creates a security concern for member-states and potentially hinders economic integration. There are "illegal" Sulu immigrants, often seeking livelihoods, who face daily raids and roadblocks upon entering Sabah (Asreemoro,2008). Branded as undocumented refugees, they are deported by Malaysian authorities through joint efforts involving the Royal Police, the Registration Department, and the Immigration Department (Asreemoro, 2008). This case was further elaborated through an example wherein Filipinos residing in Malaysia face potential deportation due to their undocumented status despite ancestral ties to Sabah (Pia Gutierrez, ABS-CBN News, 2023).

Today, BIMP-EAGA authorities deem pre-modern maritime trading activities illegal. These activities, including smuggling, traditional boat use such as the *bangka, lantsa,* and *kapal kayu,* and cross-border fishing, have been banned from local communities within the sub-region. According to *Joseph* (personal communication, September 14, 2022), indigenous and informal trade are susceptible to police action because they cause economic sabotage, lack proper declaration of goods, and exceed customs volume limits. Teofilo Garcia, Jr. of the Philippine News Agency (2018) reported an incident highlighting the consequences of the illegality of informal trade using a *kapal kayu* ban. The Coast Guard District Southwestern Mindanao (CGDSWM) intercepted two wooden-hulled vessels, M/L Overseas and M/L Nadeepa, en route to Maluso, Basilan province. These vessels did not have the required documentation. Apart from this, authorities confiscated contraband from these vessels, including rice and other commodities valued at a minimum of Php 33 million.

Furthermore, BIMP-EAGA regulations prohibit non-conventional vessels like *bangka, lantsa,* and *kapal kayu* within the sub-region.

Communities in Palawan and along Indonesian and Malaysian borders persist in building and using traditional wooden boats known as *kapal kayu* (Consulate General of Indonesia and Malaysia in Davao City, personal communication, 2022). Moreover, these vessels are now deemed to be "substandard" for failing to meet the maritime international standards and certifications required for navigating the area's water, as outlined by the Centre for International Law (CIL, 2018), IMO, and MOU on the *Improvement of Safety Standards and Inspection for Non-Convention Ships* within the ASEAN region. *Joseph* (personal communication, September 14, 2022) highlighted that these communities traditionally built *lantsa* for trade routes between Western Mindanao, Malaysia, and Palawan. However, BIMP-EAGA's modernization efforts continue to disrupt these practices, impacting the livelihoods of communities that have relied on them for generations.

BIMP-EAGA regulations are coupled with the favoritism shown towards large fishing companies and the prohibition of fishing among local communities in the sub-region. This stems from territorial disputes, particularly over Sabah, and the need to delineate maritime exclusive economic zones (EEZs). Governments now heavily regulate and police fishing activities within EEZs, which disrupts the traditional practices of local fisherfolks. News articles highlight the consequences of these regulations. Palicte (2019) reports on the arrest of ten Filipino fisherfolks, including a minor, by Indonesian authorities for entering their waters without proper documentation and engaging in illegal fishing, poaching, and smuggling. Escobal, one of the detained fisherfolks, narrates that their lack of proper certifications and documents led to charges of illegal fishing. Similar incidents occur throughout the sub-region.

The sub-regional integration's economic plans, particularly the role of the policymakers, hinder the sub-region's maritime development. The SMEs and MNCs are the BIMP-EAGA's key source of information on maritime activities (BIMP-EAGA, 2017). While this involvement can be valuable, it raises concerns about potential bias, as private interests may not always align with those of marginalized communities. The MNCs and SMEs, shaped by Western approaches, influence BIMP-EAGA's economic policies through their involvement in creating development plans and policy implementation. These policymakers involved in the modernization of economic plans outlined in BIMP-EAGA documents rely heavily on the private sector for support and resources to fulfill projects. One example of policymakers is the German Technical Cooperation Agency (GTZ), an agency of the German government that provides limited capital funding in various major regions in the world and technical expertise to the drafting process of the development documents of the BIMP-EAGA (BIMP-EAGA, 1995, p. 2 and Thynell, 2009).

An example of an active SME in the BIMP-EAGA is Simphor Pharma Sdn. Bhd. from Brunei Darussalam. Its standardized manufactured products leave traditional alternative medicines used by local communities to be regarded as unreliable and dangerous. In Indonesia, ICT has enabled partnerships between the government and local businesses with the Australian Trade and Investment Commission (Austrade). The MNC imparted knowledge to Indonesian business owners to transform the country's digital landscape, helping them seek potential within the Indonesian market. Sabah in Malaysia is home to the Sawit Kinabalu Group, which has a significant influence over the standards of cultivation, processing, procurement, and palm oil trade in Malaysia. This has led local communities producing palm oil to face challenges competing with the giant, commercialized operation.

Before the Westphalian concept of nation-states, the earlier or traditional activities were simply part of life. However, sovereignty issues are exacerbated as BIMP-EAGA lobbies its member-states to strengthen and modernize such policies. The Consulate General of the Republic of Indonesia and MinDA acknowledge that modernization efforts are not intended to eliminate traditional maritime practices. Instead, they aim to help these practices adapt and thrive in the modern landscape (personal communication, October 14, 2022; September 5, 2022). However, the challenges and cases outlined stem from the inherent tensions between traditional practices and the Westphalian-centric framework of governance adopted by the BIMP-EAGA, which can create tensions and barriers to economic integration within BIMP-EAGA.

BIMP-EAGA's modernization efforts and trade regulations pose significant barriers to economic integration among member states. The focus on modernization and territorial integrity exacerbates issues related to disputed territories like Sabah. These regulations and favoritism toward large conglomerate fishing companies restrict fishing activities among micro-, small and medium-sized (MSMEs) local communities. Strict border controls impede the free movement of people within the sub-region. Moreover, BIMP-EAGA's policies limit traditional practices, with authorities classifying the transfer of goods in traditional vessels as smuggling, hindering traditional trade. Standardizing maritime shipping vessels renders traditional vessels illegal, further impacting local fishers' livelihoods. Additionally, the influence of SMEs and MNCs in decision-making silences local communities, hindering their development.

Conclusions and Recommendations

The BIMP-EAGA, modeled on Western ideals, prioritizes rapid economic integration through increased accessibility, which overlooks the sub-region's rich pre-modern maritime trade activities. Analyzing these practices through the lens of Quijano's Colonial Matrix of Power exposes how lingering colonial influences, embedded in BIMP-EAGA's policies that are modeled after Western notions of nation-states, disrupt traditional trade activities and exacerbate resource disparities. As revealed in this study, pre-modern maritime trade activities were built on networks of alliances, barter systems, and thriving river routes flourished within the sub-region. However, these practices are now marginalized by BIMP-EAGA's Western-centric economic development policies. Additionally, policymakers' perceptions are demonstrably dominated by Western paradigms as evident in their rationalization of modernization initiatives, such as enhancing CIQS and digitizing mechanisms through ICT. The initiatives raise concerns about the future of the BIMP-EAGA subregion and its traditional maritime trade.

With the findings, the researchers forward certain policy and academic research recommendations. First, this study urges BIMP-EAGA and government institutions to create people-centric approaches, such as development plans and policies focused on marginalized traditional maritime communities. This shift requires moving away from Westernized and colonial perceptions of modernization and embracing culturally sensitive approaches for effective sub-regional integration. The researchers also suggest enriching the study by expanding the informant pool, especially from the representative offices and informants from Brunei Darussalam. Lastly, the proponents of this study recommend the usage of Quijano's Sphere of Gender, which will analyze how gender issues impact economic development plans within the sub-region. All these recommendations guide BIMP-EAGA in navigating its future to anchor firmly with its core objectives amidst the waves of progress.

Acknowledgements

We extend our sincerest gratitude to our thesis mentor, Ms. Monica A. Villa Abrille, M.A., for her unwavering support and patience during our entire research-making journey. Also, we are grateful to our thesis adviser, Mr. John Harvey D. Gamas, M.A., and panelists Mr. Jose C. Enrique Sibala, MILIR, and Ms. Krizza Janica B. Mahinay, M.A., for their guidance in completing this research. Finally, we thank the Lord for giving us the grace of strength to accomplish this research.

References

Abinales, P. & Amoroso, D. (2017). *State and Society in the Philippines* (2nd ed.). Rowman & Littlefield.

Adelaar, T. (2000). Electronic Commerce and the Implications for Market Structure: The Example of the Art and Antiques Trade. *Journal of Computer-Mediated Communication, 5(3).* https://doi.org/10.1111/j.1083-6101.2000.tb00346.x

Andaya, L. (2002). Orang Asli and the Melayu in the History of the Malay Peninsula. *Journal of the Malaysian Branch of the Royal Asiatic Society, 75(1), 23-48.* https://www.jstor.org/stable/41493461

Arhem, K. (2016). *Animism in Southeast Asia* (1ˢᵗ ed.). Routledge Taylor & Francis Group.

Asian Development Bank. (2006). *BIMP-EAGA Roadmap to Development 2006-2010*.https://www.adb.org/sites/default/files/related/19736/bimp-eaga-roadmap-development-2006-2010.pdf

Asreemoro, & Ahmad, A. B. (2008). Tausug & the Sulu Sultanate. Saba Islamic Media.

Aung-Thwin, M. (2014). Nationalism and Post-Colonial identity in Southeast asia. *Routledge Handbook of Southeast Asian History, 51*(09), 75–85. https://doi.org/10.4324/9780203763117.ch8

Balassa, B. (1994). The Theory of Economic Integration: An Introduction. Greenwood Publishing Group. *Journal of African Economies, 28(1), 89–118.* https://doi.org/10.1093/jae/ejy016

Bangko Sentral ng Pilipinas. (n.d.). *Coins and notes - history of Philippine money*. BSP. Retrieved March 19, 2022, from https://www.bsp.gov.ph/Pages/CoinsAndNotes/HistoryOfPhilippineMoney/HistoryOfPhilippineMoney.aspx#:%7E:text=Long%20before%20the%20Spaniards%20came,of%20exchange%20%E2%80%93%20the%20cowry%20shells.

Baumann, H. (2021). Avatars of Eurocentrism in International Political Economy Textbooks: The Case of the Middle East and North Africa. *Politics, 20(1).* https://journals.sagepub.com/toc/pol/0/0

Bausani, A. (1960). The First Italian-Malay Vocabulary by Antonio Pigafetta. *East and West, 11*(4), 229–248. http://www.jstor.org/stable/29754279

BIMP-EAGA. (2009). *BIMP-EAGA Roadmap to Development 2006-2010.* https://www.adb.org/sites/default/files/related/19736/bimp-eaga-roadmap-develop

BIMP-EAGA. (2017). *BIMP-EAGA vision 2025.* https://bimp-eaga.asia/sites/default/files/publications/bimp-eaga-vision-2025.pdf

Borschberg, P. (2020). The Melaka Empire, c. 1400-1528. Empire of the Sea: Maritime Power Networks in World History. Brill Publishing.

Cain, T. A. (2015). Rebuild or Reform: Regional and Subregional Architecture in the Pacific Island Region. *Journal of Societies and Oceanists, (pp. 49-48).* https://doi.org/10.4000/jso.7246a

Chang, W. & Tagliacpzzp, E. (2011). *Capital, Commodities, and Networks in Southeast Asia.* Duke University Press.

Cheok, C.K. & Chen, Y.C. (2019). Assessing ASEAN's Relevance: Have the Right Questions Been Asked? *Journal of Southeast Asian Economies, 36(1), 11-24.* https://www.jstor.org/stable/26664250

Chia, S. Y. (2013). The ASEAN Economic Community: Progress, Challenges, and Prospects. *Asian Development Bank Institute Working Paper Series. Article no. 440.* https://think-asia.org/handle/11540/1202

Dellios, R. (2003). Mandala: From sacred Origins to Sovereign Affairs in Traditional Southeast Asia. *East-West Cultural and Economic Studies, 8(10)*. https://pure.bond.edu.au/ws/portalfiles/portal/28738047/Mandala_from_sacred_origins.pdf

Dent, C. M., & Richter, P. (2011). Contemporary Southeast Asia. *Sub-Regional Cooperation and Developmental Regionalism: The Case of BIMP-EAGA, 33*(01), 29–55. https://www.jstor.org/stable/41288814

Diamond, P. (2019). The great globalization disruption: Democracy, capitalism, and inequality in the industrialized world. *The crisis of globalization: Democracy, capitalism, and inequality in the twenty-first century*, 1-24.

Dorn, J.A. (2007). Sustainable Development: A Market-Liberal Vision. *The Electronic Journal of Sustainable Development, 1(1), 1-27*. https://dlc.dlib.Indiana.edu/dlc/bitstream/handle/10535/2673/SUSTAINABLE_DEVELOPMENT_A_MARKET-LIBERAL_VISION.pdf?sequence=1&isAllowed=y

Gamas, J. H. D. (2020). Butuan in the pre-colonial Southeast Asian international system. In F.A. Cruz & N.M. Adiong (Eds.), *International studies in the Philippines: Mapping new frontiers in theory and practice*. Taylor & Francis.

Garcia, T. (2018, August 27). PCG seizes 2 boats loaded with smuggled rice off basilan. Philippine News Agency. Retrieved January 16, 2024, from https://www.pna.gov.ph/articles/1046091

Hall, K. (1985). *Maritime Trade and State DEvelopment in Early Southest Asia*. University of Hawai'i Press. https://doi.org/10.2307/j.ctv9zckps

Hayase, Shinzo (2007). Mindanao Ethnohistory Beyond Nations. Maguindanao, Sangir, and Bagobo Societies in East Maritime Southeast Asia. Ateneo de Manila University Press.

Healey, C. J. (1985). Tribes and States in "Pre-colonial" Borneo: Structural contradictions and the generation of piracy on JSTOR. Social Analysis: The International Journal of Anthropology, 18, 3–39. https://www.jstor.org/stable/23169340

Hiratsuka, D. & Kimura, F. (Eds.). (2008). *East Asia's Economic Integration: Progress and Benefit*. Palgrave Macmillan.

Hopkins F. G. (1912). Feeding experiments illustrating the importance of accessory factors in normal dietaries. *The Journal of physiology, 44*(5-6), 425–460. https://doi.org/10.1113/jphysiol.1912.sp001524

Huntington, S. P. (2000). *The Clash of Civilizations?. In Culture and Politics*. Palgrave Macmillan, New York

Hutterer, K. (1977). Economic Exchange and Social Interaction in Southeast Asia: Perspectives from Prehistory, History, and Ethnography. University of Michigan. https://hdl.loc.gov/loc.gdc/gdcebookspublic.2020749622

Jeppie S. (1987). *Historical Process and the Constitution of Subjects: The Reinvention of the Malay*. University of Cape Town.

Junker, L. (1999). *Raiding, Trafing, and Feating: The Political Economy of Philippine Chiefdoms.* University of Hawai'i Press.

Kawai, M. (2004). *Regional Economic Integration and Cooperation in East Asia.* https://www.oecd.org/gov/pcsd/33628756.pd

Kian, K. (2013). Chinese Economic Dominance in Southeast Asia: A "Longue Duree" Perspective. *Comparative Studies in Society and History, 55(1), 5-34.* https://www.jstor.org/stable/23526400

Kraugman & Obstel, (2003). International Economics: Theory and Policy. https://edisciplinas.usp.br/pluginfile.php/176676/mod_resource/content/1/KRUGMAN.pdf

Latiff, H. & Hassan, A. (2009). *Corporate social responsibility of Islamic financial institutions and businesses. Optimizing charity value, Humanomics, Vol. 25 No. 3, pp. 177-188.* https://doi.org/10.1108/08288660910986900o

Majul, C. A. (1966). *The role of Islam in the history of the Filipino people.* Dansalan Research Center.

Manggala, P. U. (2013). The Mandala Culture of Anarchy: The Pre-Colonial Southeast Asian International Society. *Journal of ASEAN Studies, 1(1), 1-13.* https://www.neliti.com/publications/26974/the-mandala-culture-of-anarchy-the-pre-colonial-southeast-asian-international-so

Mignolo, W. D. (2007a). Coloniality and modernity/rationality. *Cultural Studies, 21*(2–3), 168–178. https://doi.org/10.1080/09502380601164353

Mignolo, W. D. (2007b). Delinking. *Cultural Studies, 21*(02), 449–514. https://doi.org/10.1080/09502380601162647

Mignolo, W. (2008). *The Geopolitics of Knowledge and The Colonial Difference.* In M. Moraña, E. Dussel, & C. A. Jáuregui (Eds.), Coloniality at large: Latin America and the postcolonial debate (pp. 235–258). Durkham, NC: Duke University Press.

Murray, P. (2011). Ideas of regionalism: The European Case. *Japanese Journal of Political Science, 12(2), 305-322.* https://doi.org/10.1017/S1468109911000090

Muramatsu, M. and Krauss, S. (1987). "The Conservative Policy Line and the Development of Patterned Pluralism." In *The Political Economy of Japan: the Domestic Transformation,* ed. K. Yamamura and Y. Yasuba. Stanford, CA: Standford University Press, 516-54.

Najtama, F. (2018). Perkembangan Islam Di Brunei. *Tasamuh: Jurnal Studi Islam, 10*(2), 407–421. https://doi.org/10.32489/tasamuh.44

Nicholl, R. (1983). Brunei Rediscovered: A Survey of Early Times. *Journal of Southeast Asian Studies, 14(1), 32-45.* http://www.jstor.org/stable/20174317

Popović, G. (2010). Theory and Practice of Regional Economic Integrations. *Theory and Practice of Regional Economic Integrations, 2(57), (155-173).* https://ageconsearch.umn.edu/record/245124/files/Article%201.pdf

Pye, L. W., Pye, M. W., & Pye, L. W. (2009). Asian Power and politics: The Cultural Dimensions of Authority. Harvard University Press.

Qian, W. (1995). The United Nations and State Sovereignty in the Post-Cold War Era. *Pacifica Review: Peace, Security & Global Change, 7(2), 135-146.* doi:10.1080/14781159508412807

Quijano, A., & Ennis, M. (2000). Nepantla: Views from south. *Coloniality of Power, Eurocentrism, and Latin America, 1*(3), 533–580. https://edisciplinas.usp.br/pluginfile.php/347342/mod_resource/content/1/Quijano%20(2000)%20Colinality%20of%20power.pdf

Quijano, A. (2000a). Coloniality of power and eurocentrism in latin america. *International Sociology, 15*(2), 215–232. https://doi.org/10.1177/0268580900015002005

Quijano, A. (2000b). *Modernidad y democracia: Intereses y conflictos* (12th ed., Vol. 12). de próxima publicación en Anua.

Quijano, A. (2007). Coloniality and modernity/rationality. *Cultural Studies, 21*(2–3), 168–178. https://doi.org/10.1080/09502380601164353

Quimba, F. M. A., & Barral, M. A. A. (2019). *The Evolution of APEC and its Role in the Philippine Trade and Investment* (No. 2019-07). PIDS Discussion Paper Series.

Rafferty, E. (1984). Languages of the Chinese of Java: An Historical Review. *The Journal of Asian Studies, 43(2), 247–272.* https://doi.org/10.2307/2055313

Rana, P. B. (2012). Regional Economic Integration in Asia: Historical and Contemporary Perspectives. Renaissance of Asia: Evolving Economic Relations Between South Asia and East Asia, 13.

Reid, A. (1988). *Southeast Asia in the Age of Commerce, 1450-1680.* Yale University Press.

Reid, A. (1990). An 'Age of Commerce' in Southeast Asian History. *Modern Asian Studies, 24(1), 1-30.* http://www.jstor.org/stable/312501?origin=JSTOR-pdf

Robequain, C., & Laborde, E. D. (1969, December 31). *Malaya Indonesia Borneo and the Philippines: A Geographical, Economic and Political Description of Malaya, the East Indies, and the Philippines* (Reprint). Longmans, Green and Co.

Saleeby, N. M. B. (1908). *The History of Sulu - 1870* [E-book]. Legare Street Press. Retrieved March 10, 2022, from https://www.gutenberg.org/ebooks/41771.epub.images?session_id=41b1aae348241dc26d05077cb590a3312f8a5307

Smith, K. E., Bátora, J., & Tonra, B. (2018). The European Union in the world: Actors and policies in a changing global environment. Palgrave Macmillan.

Smith, L. T. (1999). *Decolonizing methodologies: research and indigenous peoples.* London and Dunedin: Zed Books/University of Otago Press.

Söderbaum, F. (2013). Rethinking Regions and Regionalism. Georgetown Journal of International Affairs, 14(2), 9–18. http://www.jstor.org/

stable/43134407 Too

Sutherland, H. (2003). Southeast Asian History and the Mediterranean Analogy. *Journal of southeast Asian Studies, 34(1), 1-20.* https://www.jstor.org/stable/20072472

Sutherland, H. (2021). *Seaways and Gatekeepers: Trade and State in the Eastern Archipelagos of Southeast Asia, c. 1600-c. 1906.* National Universisty of Singapore.

Telò, M. (2020). *Regional Organizations and Inter-regional Relations: Competitive Models or a Bottom-up Changes of Multilateral Global Governance.* https://doi.org/10.4000/belgeo.43943

Thambipillai, P. (1998). Brunei Darussalam and ASEAN: Regionalism for a small state. Asian Journal of Political Science, 6(1), 80–94. https://doi.org/10.1080/02185379808434116

Tooker, D. (1996). Putting the Mandala in its Place: A Practice-based Approach to the Spatialization of Power on the Southeast Asian 'Periphery'—The Case of the Akha. The Journal of Asian Studies, 55(2), 323-358. doi:10.2307/2943362

Traube, E. (1989). Review of Cosmology and Social Life: Ritual Exchange AMong the Mambai of East Timor. *Journal of Southeast Asian Studies, 20(01), 126-128.* http://dx.doi.org/10.1017/S0022463400020002

Turner, M. & Kühn, F. P. (2016). *The Politics of International Intervention: The Tyranny of Peace.* Routledge.

Veg, S. (2019). The rise of China's statist intellectuals: Law, sovereignty, and "Repoliticization". *The China Journal, 82* (1), 23-45. https://www.journals.uchicago.edu/doi/abs/10.1086/702687?mobileUi=0&journalCode=tcj

Waisberg, T. (2017). The Treaty of Tordesillas and The Re-Invention of International Law in the Age of Discovery. *Journal of Global Studies, (47).* http://doi.org/10.20889/M47e18003

Warren, J. (1981). The Sulu Zone, 1768-1898: The Dynamics of External Trade, Slavery, and Ethnicity in the Transformation of a Southeast Asian Maritime state. https://ci.nii.ac.jp/ncid/BB00850560

Warren, J. F. (2002). *Iranun and Balangingi: Globalization, Maritime Raiding, and the Birth of Ethnicity.* NUS Press.

Warren, J. F. (2007). *The Sulu Zone, 1768-1898: The Dynamics of External Trade, Slavery, and Ethnicity in the Transformation of a Southeast Asian Maritime State.* NUS Press.

Warren, J. F. (2008). *Pirates, Prostitutes, and Pullers: Explorations in the Ethno-and Social History of Southeast Asia.* UWA Press.

Winzeler, R. (1983). The Study of Malay Magic. *Bijdragen tot de Taal-, Land- en Volkenkunde, 139(4), 435-458.* https://www.jstor.org/stable/27863530

Wolters, O. W. (1982). *History, Culture, and Region in Southeast Asian Perspec-*

tives. Cornell University Press.

Wolters, O. W. (1999). *History, Culture, and Region in Southeast Asian Perspectives* (REV-Revised, 2). Cornell University Press. http://www.jstor.org/stable/10.7591/j.ctv3s8sdd

X-Border Local Research Network. (2019, August). *Trade in the sulu archipelago: Informal economies amidst maritime security challenges.* Asia Foundation. https://asiafoundation.org/publication/trade-in-the-sulu-archipelago-informal-economies-amidst-maritime-security-challenges/

Yap, J. T. & Rosellon, M. A. D. (2012). *The Role of the Private Sector in Regional Economic Integration: A View from the Philippines.* https://www.researchgate.net/publication/254441758_The_Role_of_the_Private_Sector_in_Regional_Economic_Integration_a_View_from_the_Philippines

Zhao, Z. (2015). Closing a sociodemographic chapter of Chinese history. Population and Development Review, 41(4), 681–686. https://doi.org/10.1111/j.1728-4457.2015.00090.x

Zreik, M. (2021). The Westphalia Peace and Its Impact on the Modern European State. *Quantum Journal of Social Science and Humanities, 2(1), 1-16.* https://media.neliti.com/media/publications/348773-the-westphalia-peace-and-its-impact-on-t-2457df08.pdf

Chapter 4

Unhappy Securitization: The U.S. Deportation "Regime" During the Obama Administration

Christabel Erica L. Nicolas, Kathryn Marlowe A. Lomogdang, & Joice Jonah F. Esteron

ABSTRACT

Unhappy Securitization delineates the character of the US deportation regime during the Obama administration, highlighting the disparity between its intended objectives and actual results achieved. Upon assuming the presidency, Barack Obama adhered to democratic ideals of strengthening the US immigration system. However, his tenure earned him the moniker "deporter-in-chief" from immigrant advocacy groups due to the continuation of deportation practices. To reconcile this apparent paradox with his Democratic political stance, the researchers utilized Rita Floyd's Revised Securitization Theory to understand the underlying intention and sincerity behind the securitizing practices enacted under the guise of national security. It was identified that President Obama aimed to securitize the referent objects, encompassing the natural-born US citizens; legal migrants and immigrants; and undocumented immigrants from the threat of the "broken immigration system". The researchers examined US official publications of speech acts, immigration policies and programs, the enforcement of laws by various agencies and federal departments, interviews with natural-born Americans, legal migrants, and undocumented immigrants were also conducted. The findings revealed that despite efforts, the Obama administration (2009-2017) fell short in completely alleviating the referent objects from the identified existential threat posed by the "broken immigration system". The researchers concluded that the Obama administration benefited from the securitization process rather than the referent objects themselves.

Keywords: *Revised Securitization Theory, Obama administration, US immigration system, US deportation regime*

Introduction

When Barack Obama was elected President of the US on a platform of hope and change, he promised a more humane approach to immigration policy (Tolbert, 2010). During Obama's administration, initiatives were implemented to streamline the immigration system and manage irregular migration flows through the US deportation regime as a tool for securitizing. However, his efforts to reform the immigration system and deport undocumented immigrants prompted a significant controversy among immigrant communities and US citizens. In this study, securitizations can be unhappy when security referents, the beneficiaries of the securitization practice, are not secured from the perceived threat. Consequently, the researchers explored the political objectives and the intentions of the US deportation regime during Obama's administration to determine the sincerity and consistency behind US immigration. Since the administration's efforts to securitize and alleviate the referent objects from the existential threat were unsuccessful, it is arguably a case of an unhappy securitization. Although the Obama administration securitized the referent objects, there were inconsistencies in its US deportation regime.

Delving deeper into the complexities of immigration patterns, scholars emphasized the two factors that affect immigration flow to the United States. This includes the importance of understanding the "push factors" that drive individuals to migrate from their home country and "pull factors" that attract immigrants to move to the US particularly in terms of political, economic, and social aspects. Firstly, the push factors for the majority of immigrants in the US are undesirable economic conditions, environmental displacement and political oppression. Secondly, the pull factors for US immigrants are due to geographical proximity for most Latino immigrants, abundant economic opportunities, and a foundation of political stability (Bansak et al., 2015). These are factors that affect immigration flow to the United States. In receiving immigrants in the US, American nativist sentiments, racialization and exclusion of immigrants in the United States influenced the construction of immigration laws. Meanwhile, scholarly debates on immigration emphasize how criminal law has been infused into immigration law which has perpetuated the framing of undocumented immigrants as "illegal immigrants" and "criminal aliens" (Valdez, 2016). Scholarly literature on undocumented immigrants in the United States traces how the undocumented immigrant population increased throughout the years and how immigrant reception is affected by the political landscape in the United States. Altogether, these factors consequently shape the US immigration system.

Numerous studies on the analyses of the US deportation regime delineate how deportation began as a fragmented policy in the 19th century, which compounded as a form of state control that aims to address the influx of undocumented immigrants and removal of "criminal aliens" or undocumented immigrants. Scholarly debates on immigration highlight how "crimmigration" has perpetuated the negative image of illegal immigrants and "criminal aliens" (Lai & Lasch, 2017). The history of the undocumented immigrants in the United States highlighted how the US relied mostly on immigrant labor provided by undocumented immigrants. Changes in the recent demographics of undocumented immigrants in the US were also discussed. Studies on the US deportation regime focus on the justification of sovereignty, detention, and the category of "deportability" concomitantly creates the "illegal" status of immigrants (De Genova, 2002).

Despite the gathered scholarly literature on deportation laws, there are limitations on the scope of its discussion, particularly the motives and implications of presidential administrations in shaping the US deportation regime. The subsequent impact and consistency of the president's programs and initiatives are also not discussed, including how the US Department of Homeland Security (DHS) has propelled the US deportation regime. Thus, it is imperative to examine the experiences of those who were affected by the US deportation regime during the Obama administration and the changes that were implemented. Hence, this study seeks to examine how the Obama administration securitized undocumented immigrants, legal immigrants, and natural-born US citizens through the US deportation regime. Moreover, the consistencies and inconsistencies of the US deportation regime under the Obama administration were also scrutinized while aiming to explore how it resulted in an unhappy securitization.

The theory used in this study is the Revised Securitization Theory (RST) by Rita Floyd which emphasized three theoretical concepts: (1) securitization; (2) the intentions of the securitizing actors; and (3) the beneficiaries of the securitization practices (Floyd, 2010). RST principles were employed to analyze speech acts, security measures, referent objects' responses and observations, and the immigration agencies' intentions in the Obama administration's securitizing practice. In order to examine whether the Obama administration securitized the referent objects, namely the natural-born US citizens, legal immigrants, and undocumented immigrants. The RST was used to ascertain whether the Obama administration was consistent in securitizing these three referent objects. The researchers contend that the Obama administration employed speech acts and securitizing practices for US undocumented migrants, legal migrants, and natural-born US citizens utilizing the US deportation regime. The Obama administration sought to maintain a consistent approach to security measures, but faced challenges in implementing these measures due to the influence of political actors and opposition parties within the administration. As a result, the administration's efforts to secure the objects of concern were ultimately unsuccessful, concluding that this is a case of an unhappy securitization.

This study covers 2009 to 2017, encompassing the two terms of President Obama; distinguished by the rise of deportation rates and the deliberations surrounding policies related to the movement of people across borders. The researchers employed qualitative descriptive research methodology through in-depth interviews to provide a platform for respondents to express and elaborate on their own narratives. A total of 35 individuals participated in the interviews, 17 were natural-US born citizens, 15 of whom were legal immigrants, and 3 of whom were illegal immigrants. The interviews were conducted via Google Forms, Twitter, Instagram, and various other online platforms. To protect the identity of the respondents, aliases were assigned to each of them. The researchers also looked at Presidential speeches and government policies to ascertain the speech acts and securitizing practices.

The Obama Administration's Securitization Practice

Securitization consists of two events: (1) the securitizing move and (2) security practice. A securitization exists only at the point when: (1) the existential threat justification is complemented by (2) a discernible change in behavior by the relevant agent, which is linked to the declared threat (Floyd, 2010). The Obama administration securitized the natural-born US citizens, legal migrants and immigrants, and undocumented immigrants through speech acts, immigration policies and programs, and enforcement of law by immigration agencies and federal departments. President Obama in his speeches first identified the existential threats to the three referent objects. Then the discussion is followed by the administration's initiatives on immigration policies and programs to securitize the three referent objects. Lastly, the securitizing moves were accomplished through the enforcement of law by immigration agencies in the US. The Obama administration used the US deportation regime as a tool to securitize the referent objects; however, it resulted in protectionist policies, legal changes, and mass deportations of both undocumented and legal migrants and immigrants.

The US deportation regime during the Obama's administration can be distinguished into two periods of immigration enforcement. The first period, which is from 2009 to 2011, saw high levels of US Immigration and Customs Enforcement (ICE) arrests and the execution of immediate removals by the end of the Bush administration; During the second period, from 2012 to 2016, new enforcement priorities and prosecutorial discretion policies narrowed the scope of enforcement activities, leading to sharp declines in arrests and removals (US Immigration and Customs Enforcement, 2015). A number of states passed laws supporting pro-enforcement legislation during Obama's first term, including Georgia and Tennessee in 2009. Arizona passed SB 1070 in 2010, the most widely circulated and comprehensive pro-enforcement state law at that time. Subsequently, similar laws were approved in Utah, Alabama, Indiana, and South Carolina. Laws with more stringent provisions on immigration enforcement were established in Tennessee, Oklahoma, and Georgia (Capps et al., 2020). Although immigration laws in Arizona attracted the most attention, Migration Policy Institute researchers discovered that immigrants were often arrested in other states like Florida, Georgia, North Carolina, and South Carolina for traffic violations and other minor infractions (Shahshahani, 2009).

The Obama administration implemented various immigration policies and programs aimed at enhancing public safety for natural-born US citizens. Key initiatives included the Southern Border Approach & Campaign Plan (SBACP), New Deportation Priorities for US Immigration and Customs Enforcement (ICE) and US Customs and Border Protection (CBP), and the replacement of the Secure Communities (SCP) with the Priority Enforcement Program (PEP). The SBACP, established in May 2014 under the DHS, prioritized removal actions for undocumented immigrants based on comprehensive agency-wide strategies. Additionally, ICE issued memos in 2011 and 2012 outlining enforcement priorities, focusing on individuals with felony convictions, multiple misdemeanor offenses, or significant threats to public safety. The implementation of these priorities commenced in 2015, emphasizing prosecutorial discretion based on factors such as residency duration and familial connections. Collaboration between ICE and local law enforcement agencies aimed to identify and remove criminal aliens, with a focus on individuals involved in violent or property crimes. Funding requests for enforcement initiatives included resources for detention beds, alternatives to detention programs, fugitive tracking, and removal operations targeting criminal aliens. These measures underscored the administration's commitment to enforcing immigration laws, prioritizing public safety concerns for US citizens (A Review of the Department of Homeland Security's Policies and Procedures for the Apprehension, Detention, and Release of Noncitizens Unlawfully Present in the United States,

2015).

The administration extended security concerns to legal immigrants by highlighting the challenges posed by illegal immigrants. Obama emphasized in his speeches how the influx of illegal immigrants undermined the efforts of those pursuing legal immigration processes (Obama, 2010). He underscored the economic contributions of legal immigrants, particularly as entrepreneurs, researchers, and students, but lamented how the broken immigration system hindered their potential and posed challenges to the state. In addressing Republicans, Obama expressed frustration over the obstruction to immigration reform, which he argued would have fixed the system and enhanced border security. He criticized the consequences of this obstruction, including the exploitation of illegal workers by companies and the departure of skilled immigrants, leading to competition with American companies and workers (Obama, 2014). Obama highlighted the plight of 11 million immigrants living in the shadows, unable to gain citizenship and causing distress among separated families. These speeches illustrate the administration's efforts to address the complexities of immigration policy and the impact on legal immigrants amidst broader security concerns.

The Obama administration also implemented measures to address concerns faced by legal immigrants, aiming to modernize and streamline the immigration system. Initiatives included H-1B Spouses Work Authorization, extension of Optional Practical Training (OPT) for foreign STEM students, and National Interest Waivers for investors, researchers, and entrepreneurs (US Citizenship and Immigration Services, 2015). Additionally, efforts were made to promote naturalization and clarify eligibility criteria for green card applicants, particularly under the EB-2 category. Legislative proposals such as the Comprehensive Immigration Reform for America's Security and Prosperity (CIR ASAP) Act of 2009 were introduced to address comprehensive immigration reform, although they faced challenges in Congress (US Citizenship and Immigration Services Ombudsman, 2017). In terms of enforcement, the DHS focused on prosecuting employers who knowingly hired illegal immigrants through worksite enforcement programs. Collaboration between federal, state, and local law enforcement agencies was facilitated through initiatives like the ICE 287(g) Program, allowing for joint efforts to enforce immigration laws and address national security concerns. These efforts aimed to enhance transparency, flexibility, and accountability within the immigration system, ensuring the safety and security of the nation (US Immigration and Customs Enforcement, 2010).

During the Obama administration, undocumented immigrants were a focal point of immigration policy discussions. President Obama emphasized the need for comprehensive immigration reform to address issues within the immigration system, including pathways to legal status for undocumented immigrants. He championed the protection of undocumented immigrants, particularly advocating for "Dreamers" and prioritizing deportation for felons over families (Obama, 2013). However, efforts to pass comprehensive immigration reform faced obstacles in Congress due to the opposition from some Republicans. In response, Obama announced executive actions to change immigration policies, extending protection from deportation to certain undocumented immigrants, including Deferred Action for Childhood Arrivals (DACA) recipients and skilled workers (Obama, 2014).

Regardless of record statistics on immigration enforcement, including the removal of aliens convicted of crimes, the Obama administration's efforts to fix the immigration system faced challenges. DHS Secretary Janet Napolitano and US Director of Immigration and Customs Enforcement (ICE), John Morton, announced that previous records on immigration enforcement were surpassed with the dramatic increase in the total number of deported aliens in fiscal year 2010. The record is not limited to aliens convicted of crimes. The announcements delivered by Secretary Napolitano correspond with the administration's concerted effort on efficient immigration enforcement for the past 18 months since Obama's inauguration as President, with a focus on identifying and removing criminal aliens who threaten public safety (Office of the Press Secretary, 2010).

Various immigration policies and legislations were also introduced during the Obama administration to address the challenges faced by undocumented immigrants in the United States. President Obama implemented executive actions such as the DACA program, which provided temporary relief from deportation to certain young individuals who entered the country without documentation as minors. Additionally, the Deferred Action for Parents of Americans and Lawful Permanent Residents (DAPA) program aimed to protect the parents of US citizens and lawful permanent residents from deportation. However, legal challenges, particularly from Texas and other states, led to the suspension of these programs (American Immigration Council, 2021). The Obama administration also introduced the Provisional Waiver Program (I-601A waiver), allowing unauthorized spouses and children of lawful permanent residents to apply for waivers of unlawful presence while remaining in the United States. Furthermore, parole in place was expanded to provide temporary protection from deportation to family members of US military personnel (US Department of Homeland Security Press Office, 2013).

In terms of enforcement, the administration implemented the PEP, which focused on targeting individuals who posed national security threats or had been convicted of serious crimes for deportation (Vaughan, 2015). The Criminal Alien Program (CAP) continued under the Obama administration, identifying and processing undocumented immigrants with criminal records for removal (Kandel, 2016). Border security efforts were also intensified, with programs such as the Mexican Interior Repatriation Program (MIRP) and Operation Streamline aimed at deterring illegal border crossings (US Customs and Border Protection, 2010). Even with these efforts, challenges persisted, particularly with the influx of women and children from Central America fleeing poverty and violence.

The Obama administration sought to balance enforcement

measures with humanitarian considerations in its approach to immigration policy (Johnson, 2017). However, the Obama administration's securitization resulted in millions of deportations, increased border security measures, and there were also remarkable inconsistencies between rhetoric and outcomes. Although removal of criminal aliens were prioritized, there were cases of non-criminal immigrants caught in enforcement actions. Moreover, the gap between rhetoric advocating for comprehensive immigration reform and the failure to achieve bipartisan support in Congress raised questions about the effectiveness and coherence of the administration's approach. The securitization of immigration policy under the Obama administration reflected a complex interplay between political rhetoric, policy initiatives, and enforcement actions. Framing immigration as a security issue allowed for the consolidation of enforcement efforts but it also raised concerns about the impact on immigrant communities and the coherence of the administration's approach.

The Obama administration employed securitization practices, utilizing speech acts, policy implementations and enforcements by the agencies to securitize natural-born US citizens, legal migrants, and undocumented immigrants. Presidential speeches highlighted immigration policies and programs including the Southern Border Approach & Campaign Plan and the PEP aimed at enhancing public safety. Efforts extended to legal immigrants, emphasizing economic contributions while lamenting obstacles to legal immigration processes and to undocumented immigrants such as DACA and DAPA. Despite initiatives, challenges persisted leading to some program suspensions. Enforcement measures like the Priority Enforcement Program and the Criminal Alien Program targeted individuals posing national security threats or with criminal records, alongside intensified border security efforts. Hence, inconsistencies between rhetoric and outcomes including cases of non-criminal immigrants affected by enforcement actions underscores the need for a nuanced understanding of the interplay between political rhetoric, policy initiatives, and enforcement actions in the securitization of immigration and whether these referent objects were alleviated from the threat.

The Consistencies and Inconsistencies of the Obama Administration's Deportation "Regime"

Following Rita Floyd's RST, the ensuing analysis was based on two conditions: sincerity and consistency through the speech acts and if this was followed by the security practices through immigration policies and initiatives. If either of these conditions are not fulfilled, it is considered as a case of an unhappy securitization. Floyd's RST posits that the characteristic of unhappy securitization is manifested if there is a discrepancy or gap between the security move, that is, the speech acts and the security practices which is reflected in the policies and agencies. In order to look for the discrepancy, Floyd stated that it is necessary to identify whether the securitization was consistent or inconsistent on its own terms. According to Floyd's (2010) RST, consistency is characterized by the absence of behavioral change of securitizing actors or by being consistent with the threats the securitizing actors themselves identified.

In the first section it was shown how Obama's speech acts were successfully executed on the referent objects: (1) legal immigrants, (2) natural-born US citizens, and (3) undocumented immigrants. However, the securitizing move or the speech act, was not always consistent with the security practice or the implementation of the policies and programs. Thus, it is conceivable that such inconsistency exists. Hence, this second section of the study explored the inconsistencies of the US deportation regime under the Obama administration, pertaining to its programs, policies, and agencies. The analysis revealed that these inconsistencies were due to the administration's inefficient implementation of security measures, as evident in the data gathered from official US publication sites and from the interview with respondents being the referent objects of the securitization. Overall, the analysis highlights the importance of aligning security speech acts with security practices to ensure effective and legitimate securitization efforts in immigration policies and initiatives.

The Deferred Action Programs, particularly DACA, provided temporary relief from deportation to undocumented individuals brought to the US as children. DACA recipients were granted a renewable two-year period of deferred action, allowing them to live and work in the US (American Immigration Council, 2021). Two DACA recipients interviewed including Martiro (personal communication, September 25, 2023) highlighted the benefits of DACA, such as access to work permits and driver's licenses, albeit the constant fear of deportation. Additionally, the Provisional Unlawful Presence Waiver program demonstrated consistency in its objectives and eligibility criteria, leading to an increase in waiver requests. The US Citizenship and Immigration Services (USCIS) updated the program to cater to eligible applicants, expanded the extreme hardship standard, and modified form instructions. The increase in applications reflected the Obama administration's efforts to address the human toll of immigration policies and provide relief for families affected by separation (Kirchner, 2017). These initiatives showcased the Obama administration's commitment to addressing immigration challenges through executive action, notwithstanding the absence of comprehensive legislative reform.

The Obama administration's approach to immigration was also inconsistent despite its efforts to address challenges within the immigration system. These inconsistencies were evaluated based on Rita Floyd's accordance conditions, focusing on the sincerity and consistency of the administration's immigration reform efforts. During Obama's first term, there was controversy over the administration's deportation policies, with criticism focusing on the high number of deportations and the lack of progress on immigration reform legislation. While Obama had promised immigration reform, the administration faced criticism for its stringent enforcement policies, leading to a reduction in the scope of interior enforcement efforts (Gonzalez-Barrera et al., 2013). US Immigration and Customs Enforcement (ICE) Director John Morton issued memos in 2010 and 2011 limiting enforcement priorities to individuals with criminal convictions, recent arrivals, and immigration fugitives, urging agents to exercise prosecutorial discretion. The number of persons placed in ICE custody for traffic infractions decreased later in the Obama administration, suggesting a deviation from the administration's stated focus on deporting criminals posing a serious threat (Capps et al., 2018). Additionally, they suggested shortcomings in transparency, accountability, and enforcement within the DHS. Immigration officials at DHS and its predecessor, INS, had issued memoranda in 1976, 2000, 2005, and 2007 which instructed that, given the limited resources of the federal government, not every case should be pursued to deportation. Individual immigration officers and attorneys could utilize their "prosecutorial discretion" to determine which cases of arrest, detention, and deportation should be prioritized (US Immigration and Customs Enforcement, 1976; US Immigration and Customs Enforcement, 2005, US Immigration and Customs Enforcement, 2007; Immigration and Naturalization Service, 2000). In this case, it can be seen that the Obama administration was not adhering to the accordance conditions of his speech acts, which emphasizes the deportation of criminals posing a serious threat to public safety and national security.

The DACA program introduced during the Obama administration offers protection to certain undocumented immigrants from deportation and provides them with work authorization. Although there were numerous efforts to prioritize removal of individuals with criminal records, the Obama administration faced criticism for high deportation rates, leading to President Obama being dubbed as "deporter-in-chief." DACA was praised for offering temporary relief but criticized for its impermanent nature and limited scope. Interviews revealed dissatisfaction among undocumented immigrants due to fears of deportation and the inability to gain permanent legal status.

From the interviews conducted with both legal immigrants and natural-born US citizens, it was found that there is a collective dissent towards Obama's approach of equitable treatment for undocumented immigrants. Instead of alleviating deportation apprehensions and instilling confidence, this approach has led to increased skepticism due to high deportation rates. Even with initiatives like the Dreamer's Act offering a pathway to citizenship or legal residency, deportation cases remain high, causing prevalent family separation and concerns about unaccompanied undocumented children at the border. He viewed illegal immigration as a systemic issue requiring ongoing attention. Moreover, witnessing undocumented immigrants facing police scrutiny in Delaware, where they would hide or seek refuge in fear of losing everything they worked for in the United States added to his viewpoint. Additionally, Obama's failure to achieve comprehensive immigration reform through DACA highlighted the program's vulnerabilities and limited impact (American Immigration Council, 2021). Although DACA provides positive economic benefits for recipients, its inconsistencies and shortcomings underscored the challenges in aligning policy with Obama's rhetoric on inclusivity and fairness in immigration.

The DACA program is not viable for the long term given that it is an executive order under the Obama administration (2012-2017). It is important to note that the DACA program does not possess the characteristics of a legal statute and does not confer valid immigration status. One of the undocumented immigrant respondents, Martiro (personal communication, September 15, 2023), shared his sentiments regarding the impermanent nature of the DACA program:

> So out of the gate, you get a driver's license, you get a work permit, and you get a security number, which, you know, by all accounts makes you a normal person, except that you can still theoretically be deported at the DACA program where you have to come to an end. So a lot of DACA recipients, their lives change instantly, because now they can work, they can go back to school, they` could start a career, and start a family. But always, the guy said, like if the program wasn't extended, then you only have two years, and it could essentially go away a moment.

The PEP, introduced as a replacement for the Secure Communities Program during the Obama administration, aimed to rectify inconsistencies and concerns associated with its predecessor by focusing on deporting undocumented immigrants with serious criminal records. However, the program faced criticism for its lack of transparency, reliance on detainers, and potential for wrongful detentions and deportations due to data inaccuracies (Jácome, 2022). Interviews revealed dissatisfaction among undocumented immigrants and uncertainty among citizens about whether the program effectively prioritized criminals as promised. Martiro (personal communication, September 15, 2023), points out that workplace raids are "tools to create fear." Similarly, Fausto (personal communication, October 15, 2023), an undocumented immigrant has never experienced a workplace raid but witnessed the distress of many families who have. Notwithstanding Obama's rhetoric on deporting felons, the implementation of PEP faced challenges, perpetrating the fear and insecurity among immigrant communities.

Majority of the respondents from the three categories of the referent object agree that Obama did not execute all the promises he made in his speeches to prioritize "felons, not families." Martiro (personal communication, September 15, 2023), points out that workplace raids are "tools to create fear." Similarly, Fausto (personal communication, October 15, 2023), an undocumented immigrant. He recounts:

> I myself never experienced a workplace raid, but witnessed many. The cable factory my father worked at was subject to a few and our home hosted more than its fair share of crying families wondering where their breadwinner was.

Regarding apprehensions, Martiro (personal communication, September 15, 2023), was fortunate to have never been suspected as an undocumented immigrant. However, he had many friends whose parents and family members were suspected as undocumented. They experienced severe cases of apprehension by immigration authorities, which caused distrust and palpable fear towards the government that was supposed to keep them safe. Recounting from how other undocumented immigrants were apprehended, Martiro (personal communication, September 15, 2023), narrated that forced deportations were executed by immigration authorities knocking on people's doors as if they are after the "the most wanted person in the FBI's most wanted list." He emphasized that they try to deceive people by opening the doors and deporting one member or the entire family itself. Some natural-born US citizens were also uncertain whether the "felons, not families" political campaign of Obama was executed by the DHS. Melai (personal communication September 17, 2023), was unsure in answering if she believes that the "felons, not families" campaign was followed by the DHS.

The Gang of Eight bill that was initially endorsed by the Obama administration serves as a pivotal stride toward comprehensive immigration reform. However, the bill encountered hurdles within the House of the Representatives and ultimately failed to garner passage. The bill was a bipartisan legislative effort, aimed at addressing various aspects of the immigration system in the United States and encompassed sections focusing on border security, immigrant visas, interior enforcement, nonimmigrant visa programs, and youth employment (American Immigration Council, 2013). As a result, the Obama administration saw Republicans as a factor impeding legislative efforts for immigration reform. Some participants from the interview expressed frustration at their restrictive policies and perceived racism. However, others argued that Republicans were enforcing immigration laws and upholding national security. As President Obama addressed that Republican opposition in the House, led by Speaker John Boehner, further obstructed progress on immigration reform, highlighting the partisan divide on the issue (Silverleib, 2013). The respondents expressed their observations concerning Republicans as a hindrance in creating legislative efforts to address the issues in the immigration system. Aside from having a predominance of perceived racists among the Republicans, two respondents who are natural-born US citizens observed that the party seeks restrictionist policies. Eight from the natural-born US citizens out of 17 agree that Republicans were restraining legislative efforts for immigration reform. Melai (personal communication, October 17, 2023) firmly stated:

> Yes. I feel like there's a very big war against Democrats and Republicans. And I feel like Republicans are not ever satisfied with the work that the Democrat does. And they also impede some of this stuff for them to do stuff and to better it. So I do think that the Republicans do have an effect towards Democrats and stuff.

Eight from the natural-born US citizens agree that Republicans were indeed restraining legislative efforts for immigration reform. Dal (personal communication, October 15, 2023) a 56 year old Asian businessman born and raised in California, pointed out that "Republicans tend to be really strict with immigration," and can be very racist. Melai (personal communication September 17, 2023) and Mark (October 19, 2023) added that Republicans became detrimental to the political landscape of immigration in the US causing more division. He stated:

> Republicans are basically like neo-Nazis, not saying that they're overall racist but the identity of how they view other groups of people like minorities and the history of what… You know, the political party has done two different demographics is evident. A lot of Republicans hold on to ideologies that are outdated. We live in a world where everything's more modern, these more interconnected technology through shared resources, whether it's economically. I don't feel like the Republican Party has addressed the issue of immigration. I feel like they've even made it worse in some aspects.

The proposed Comprehensive Immigration Reform under Obama's administration included provisions related to border security, pathways to citizenship for undocumented immigrants, changes to visa programs, and employment verification systems. However, Obama's focus on economic recovery and healthcare legislation delayed significant action on immigration reform, with his support for reform principles only emerging in 2011. Although urging Congress for comprehensive reform in speeches, Obama faced challenges in aligning his rhetoric with results, leading to criticism for prioritizing other issues over immigration. Additionally, his administration's high deportation rates sparked accusations of inconsistency between stated priorities and actual practices regarding immigration policy.

The Obama administration aimed to address immigration

challenges through the DHS, utilizing agencies like ICE and CBP. Nevertheless, there were noted inconsistencies in the practice of legitimate deportation enforcement. Despite DHS's mission statement emphasizing safeguarding American people and values, criminal aliens were released back into communities instead of being deported, which can be attributed to both resource shortages and policy decisions. Concerns arose over the expansion of private detention facilities, which were not effectively utilized for deporting criminals as promised (US Homeland Security Advisory Council, 2016). Additionally, abuses within immigration agencies persisted, impacting immigration enforcement ideologies. The allocation of resources raised questions, with reports indicating inefficiencies and lack of accountability, particularly within CBP (Siskin & Haddal, 2010). Transparency and consistency issues were highlighted, including discrepancies in interpretation of immigration laws and varying practices at different ports of entry (Meissner & Kerwin, 2009). Stringent enforcement policies led to heightened dangers for individuals attempting illegal border crossings, despite efforts to address safety concerns (AILA-EOIR Meeting Agenda, 2010). Overall, the Obama administration's immigration efforts faced challenges aligning rhetoric with operational realities within the DHS, ICE, and CBP, showcasing the complexity of US immigration policies.

Using the RST framework revealed the inconsistency between speech acts and security practices in immigration policies under the Obama administration. While the administration demonstrated consistency in addressing challenges within the immigration system through initiatives like the Deferred Action Programs and the Provisional Unlawful Presence Waiver Program, discrepancies emerged in the implementation of deportation policies. Despite Obama's rhetoric prioritizing removal of felons over families, the deportation regime faced criticism for high deportation rates. The PEP, intended to target criminals, encountered challenges in transparency and effectiveness, contributing to fear and insecurity among immigrant communities. Moreover, the failure to achieve comprehensive immigration reform, exacerbated by Republican opposition in Congress, underscored the gap between rhetoric and action. Inconsistencies within the DHS, including resource shortages, policy decisions, and abuses, further complicated immigration enforcement efforts. Therefore, such inconsistencies from the securitization of the Obama administration highlighted a case of unhappy securitization.

The Obama Administration's Unhappy Securitization

The RST suggests that unhappy securitization occurs when security practices do not align with the speech acts announced by the securitizing actor. The Obama administration's objectives for the US deportation regime were analyzed, revealing inconsistencies in securitizing moves, security measures, and responses. The study exemplified an unhappy securitization practice, as the Obama administration failed to effectively relieve respondents from the identified existential threat. The immigration reform plan implemented by the Obama administration in the US has the potential to enhance economic growth. However, the sincerity of the actor responsible for ensuring security was not sufficient to address the existential threat. The inconsistencies between the existential threat justification and the security practice suggest that the securitizing actor has gained advantages. The Obama administration greatly benefited from Obama's implementation of securitization measures for undocumented immigrants and the inconsistent security practice demonstrated an agent benefiting securitization (ABS) rather than a referent object benefiting securitization (ROBS). The benefits of this securitization to the agent are: (1) gaining the support of Latino voters; (2) profiting private detention facilities; (3) increased employment within immigration agencies; (4) increased funds allocated to immigration agencies; and (5) the maintenance of the role of undocumented workers in the US economy's recovery. These aforementioned advantages illustrate how the administration's actions in immigration enforcement served its own interests rather than effectively addressing the perceived threats.

During the 2008 election, President Barack Obama promised Latino voters comprehensive immigration reform, but he couldn't fulfill it in his first term (Skrentny & López, 2013). Still, his proportion of the Latino vote increased in 2012 (Cook, 2012). Obama's strategic use of executive action, including the DACA program, aimed to retain and boost Latino voter support (Barreto & Segura, 2012). By focusing on deporting criminals and overturning laws separating spouses, Obama aimed to showcase the worthiness of undocumented immigrants. Romney's anti-immigration stance further solidified Latino support for Obama, with many seeing Romney as hostile or indifferent toward Hispanics. Obama's establishment of DACA before his reelection served as leverage, securing crucial support from Latino voters for his second term as President (Preston, 2012).

Private detention facilities profited from the guaranteed minimum inmate numbers, leading to a focus on maximum bed occupancy regardless of flight risk. Mandates like the "detention bed mandate" ensured a constant population that benefits for-profit companies like Corrections Corporation of America and GEO Group. Efforts to halt expansion, like the Defund Detention Campaign in Adelanto, have emerged due to concerns over inhumane conditions and abuses. Investigations into the Adelanto Detention Facility revealed complaints of extended confinement, medical neglect, limited legal assistance, religious freedom violations, physical abuse, and isolation. Accountability remains elusive, with documented cases of severe abuse and even deaths occurring within these facilities (Fialho & Mena, 2015).

During Obama's presidency, there was a notable increase in the employment of personnel within the DHS, leading to a strengthened and more capable agency (Johnson, 2017). Initiatives like the Unity of Effort initiative introduced in 2014 facilitated hiring, promotion procedures, and enhanced decision-making (Johnson, 2014). This resulted in a unified mission statement for the first time, reflecting the DHS's workforce of 232,000 employees across 22 components.

Secretary Jeh C. Johnson highlighted achievements in border security, emphasizing significant investments and advancements in technology and equipment for the Border Patrol, making it one of the largest agencies with a budget of $3.5 billion and 21,600 personnel (Johnson, 2017).

The DACA program, CAP, Secure Communities Programs, and efforts for Comprehensive Immigration Reform which target the securitization of the undocumented immigrants, received significant support from former President Barack Obama but have been subject to scrutiny due to inconsistencies. However, reports from experts and the DHS revealed that these initiatives were effective in expanding the US economy and securing greater resources for immigration authorities. Funding for immigration enforcement within the US interior has significantly increased since FY2004, with substantial allocations for programs like PEP, CAP, Secure Communities Program, 287(g), and NFOP. Congress notably raised funding levels between FY2004 to FY2006, particularly for CAP and NFOP, with ICE instructed to consider nationwide expansion of CAP in FY2006. Despite concerns about ICE's focus on deporting noncitizens who pose the most significant threats, appropriations for these programs continued to rise, illustrating an instance of agent benefiting securitization, as DHS received more funds through CAP (Kandel, 2016).

The immigration reform strategy under the Obama administration aimed at fostering economic expansion in the US. According to the Congressional Budget Office (CBO), the anticipated enactment of the Senate immigration bill led to a 3.3% increase in real Gross Domestic Product (GDP) in 2023 and a 5.4% expansion by 2033. Immigration reform was expected to enhance the employment-based green card system, attract highly skilled individuals, stimulate entrepreneurial activity, and create new enterprises, resulting in significant revenue generation and job creation. Additionally, reform aimed to harmonize family-sponsored and employment-based immigration regimes, particularly through changes to the EB-5 immigrant investor program, which would infuse capital into the economy and create job opportunities for American workers. In spite of various benefits, the primary motivation behind these immigration initiatives was seen as the economic interests of the US (The White House, 2013).

Through Floyd's RST framework it was revealed that the Obama administration's immigration policies were a case of unhappy securitization. Despite the purported intentions to alleviate existential threats, the inconsistencies between rhetoric and action reveal an ABS. The administration's actions, such as DACA implementation and deportation prioritization, aimed at securing benefits including gaining Latino voter support, profiting private detention facilities, increasing employment within immigration agencies, securing funds for enforcement, and stimulating economic recovery. While these actions aligned with the administration's interests, they failed to fully alleviate the perceived threats and provide substantial relief to the referent objects, illustrating a dissonance between stated objectives in securitization and actual outcomes in immigration policy and enforcement.

Conclusions and Recommendations

The Obama administration securitized natural-born US citizens, legal immigrants, and undocumented immigrants due to the challenges posed by the "broken immigration system," resulting in both consistencies and inconsistencies in speech acts, policies, programs, and enforcement actions. This led to a case of unhappy securitization. Obama utilized the deportation regime as a tool for securitizing referent objects, emphasizing public safety and national security but placed American communities at risk by releasing criminal aliens and mistreating detainees in private detention facilities. The Obama administration securitized natural-born Americans, legal immigrants, and illegal immigrants through security practices such as speech acts, programs and policies, and the enforcement of laws by the cabinet agencies and federal departments. Despite providing temporary relief from deportation, there were inconsistencies between Obama's presidential speech acts and the

DHS's mission statement. Obama outlined existential challenges to the immigration system, prioritizing the removal of criminals while advocating for comprehensive immigration reform, though Republican opposition hindered progress.

The administration's deportation initiatives, operated by ICE and CBP, were scrutinized in the interviews with legal immigrants, natural-born citizens, and undocumented immigrants, revealing inconsistencies in enforcement effectiveness and fairness. The US deportation "regime" was used to subject these individuals to enhanced security, contradictory to Obama's presidential addresses and DHS mission statement. The Obama administration released criminal foreigners and mistreated prisoners in private detention centers, endangering American communities. The securitization techniques affected immigrants' lives and raised concerns about immigration enforcement. Most respondents said that President Obama's immigration enforcement should have been better. They complained about immigrant mistreatment and excessive deportations. Obama's speech acts, securitization, and interview data transcripts showed that the securitization also benefited the securitizing agent and not solely the referent object. Respondents criticized high deportation numbers and perceived inconsistencies between stated goals and enforcement actions. This analysis, conducted through Floyd's RST, concludes that the Obama administration benefited from securitization instead of the referent object, demonstrated by gains among Latino voters, profits for private detention facilities, increased employment and funds for immigration agencies, and economic recovery facilitated by undocumented workers.

In conclusion, from 2009-2017, the Obama administration's US deportation regime constituted an unhappy securitization. Rita Floyd's RST effectively explains the inconsistencies in the administration's securitization practices, highlighting varying policies and programs for different referent objects, leading to differential treatment and implications of inconsistency. The securitizing actors ultimately benefited from this securitization, identifying illegal immigration as a threat but failing to thoroughly alleviate the referent objects, as indicated by reports of weak program implementation by the DHS. The consequences of this securitization were inherited by subsequent administrations. At present, the Biden administration is seeking to reverse Trump-era policies and adopt a more compassionate and humane approach to immigration.

The researchers propose doing additional studies that involve interviews with a larger sample of undocumented immigrants and DACA recipients in order to evaluate the effects of the US deportation policies implemented under the Obama administration, as well as those that were implemented by subsequent administrations. Since private detention facilities gained significant funding during Obama's tenure, research on detained immigrants is advised. The complexities of the Obama administration's immigration policies made it apparent that the pursuit of securitization yields multifaceted outcomes. Moving forward, it is essential for policymakers to engage in transparent and inclusive dialogue that considers the diverse perspectives and experiences of immigrants, while also addressing the systemic challenges embedded within the immigration system. Only through such efforts can we strive towards a more just approach to immigration policy that upholds the fundamental values of dignity and fairness regardless of their immigration status.

Acknowledgement

We express our sincere gratitude to our mentor Ms. Maria Lourdes Braceros, M.Sc., whose guidance, encouragement, and unwavering support were instrumental in the successful completion of this study. We also extend our appreciation to our research adviser, Mr. John Harvey D. Gamas, M.A., for his invaluable guidance and constructive feedback, which significantly contributed to the refinement of this work. Furthermore, we express the depths of our gratitude to our panelists, Ms. Rhisan Mae E. Morales, M.A., Ms. Rhodalie O. Emilio, M.P.A., and Ms. Monica A. Villa Abrille, M.A.S. for their insights and constructive criticisms during the evaluation process. We are grateful to everyone's dedication to academic excellence. Lastly, we would like to acknowledge the divine guidance and providence of the Lord throughout this academic journey. May His wisdom continue to illuminate our path as we embark on future endeavors.

References

American Immigration Council. (2013). *A Guide to S. 744: Understanding the 2013 Senate Immigration Bill.* https://www.americanimmigrationcouncil. org/research/guide-s744-understanding-2013-senate-immigration-bill

American Immigration Council. (2021). *Deferred Action for Childhood Arrivals (DACA)*:AnOverview:https://www.americanimmigrationcouncil. org/sites/default/files/research/deferred_action_for_childhood_arrivals_daca_an_overview_0.pdf

Bansak, C., Simpson, B. N., Zavodny, M. (2015). *The economics of immigration (1st ed.). Routledge.* https://doi.org/10.4324/9781315797250

Barreto, M. A. & Segura, M. G. (2012) *Election eve poll, Latino decisions.* https:// docs.google.com/viewer?url=http://www.latinodecisions.com/index.php/ download_file/254/213/&chrome=true.

Capps, R., Gelatt, J., Ruiz Soto, A. G., & Van Hook, J. (2020). *Unauthorized immigrants in the United States. Migration Policy Institute.* https://www. migration policy. org/sites/default/files/publications/mpi-unauthorized-immigrants-stable numbers-changingorigins_final.pdf.

De Genova, N. (2002). *Migrant illegality and deportability in everyday life.* Annual Review of Anthropology 31 (2002): 419–447.

Department of Homeland Security Appropriations Act, 2015, H.R. 240, 114th Cong. https://www.congress.gov/bill/114th-congress/house-bill/240/text.

Executive Office for Immigration Review. (2010). *AILA-EOIR Meeting Agenda. EOIR/AILA Liaison Meeting Q & A's - Archive.* US Department of Justice. https://www.justice.gov/eoir/aila-archive.

Eshbaugh-Soha, M., & Juenke, E. G. (2022). *The Politics of the President's Immigration Rhetoric.* American Politics Research ,50(1),117-130.https:// doi.org/10.1177/1532673X211042283

Fialho, C. & Mena, V. (2015). *Abuse in Adelanto: An Investigation into a California Town's Immigration Jail.* Defund Detention and Expose & Close Campaigns. http://www.endisolation.org/wp-content/uploads/2015/11/ CIVIC_DWN-Adelanto-Report_old.pdf

Floyd, R. (2010). *Security and the environment: Securitization theory and US environmental security policy.* Cambridge: Cambridge University Press. doi:10.1017/CBO9780511730146

FY2004-FY2013: US *Immigration and Customs Enforcement "Fact Sheet: Updated Facts on ICE's 287(g) Program,"* S.Rept. 108-280, S.Rept. 109-83, S.Rept. 109-273, H.Rept. 109-699, S.Rept. 110-396, S.Rept. 111-, S.Rept. 111-222, S.Rept. 109-273, H.Rept. 109-699, S.Rept. 110-396,

S.Rept. 111-31, S.Rept. 111-222, S.Rept. 112-169, P.L. 113-6, and Senate Explanatory Statement accompanying P.L. 113-6; FY2014: FY2016 DHS Budget Justification; Congressional Record, House of Representatives, January 15, 2014; FY2015: S.Rept. 111-68. FY2016-2017: DHS Congressional Budget Justification FY2017, Vol. 2, p. 3

Gonzalez-Barrera, A., Passel, J. S., D'Vera, and C., Krogstad, J. M. (2014). *As Growth Stalls, Unauthorized Immigrant Population Becomes More Settled*. Pew Research Center.https://www.pewresearch.org/race-and-ethnicity/2014/09/03/as-growth-stalls-unauthorized-immigrant-population-becomes-more-settled/

Hetherington, L (2013). Complexity Thinking and Methodology: The Potential of 'Complex Case Study' for Educational Research, Vol. 10, *Complicity: An International Journal of Complexity Theory and Education,* https://10.29173/cmplct20401.

Homeland Security Act of 2002, Pub. L. No. 107-296, §§ 441-462, 116 Stat. 2135, 2192.

Howard, W. J. (2005). ICE Principal Legal Advisor, to the Chief Counsels, *Exercising prosecutorial discretion to dismiss adjustment cases.* www.ice.gov/doclib/foia/prosecutorial-discretion/pd-dismiss-adjustment-cases.pdf

Jácome, E. (2022). *The effect of immigration enforcement on crime reporting: Evidence from Dallas. Journal of Urban Economics.* 2022. ISSN 0094-1190. https://doi.org/10.1016/j.jue.2021.103395.

Johnson, J. C. (2014). *Memo exercising prosecutorial discretion with respect to certain individuals who are the parents of US citizens or permanent residents.* Secretary of Homeland Security. https://www.dhs.gov/sites/default/files/publications/14_1120_memo_deferred_action.pdf.

Johnson, J. C. (2014). *"Strengthening departmental unity of effort," memorandum for DHS leadership.* 1.http://www.hlswatch.com/wp-content/uploads/2014/04/DHSUnityOfEffort.pdf.

Johnson, J. C. (2017). *Exit memo: Department of Homeland Security Record of progress and vision for the future.* The White House.https://obamawhitehouse.archives.gov/administration/cabinet/exit-memos/department-homeland-security

Kandel, W. A., (2016). *Interior Immigration Enforcement: Criminal Alien Programs. Library of Congress.* Congressional Research Service. https://sgp.fas.org/crs/homesec/R44627.pdf

Kirchner, J. (2017). *Annual report 2017 citizenship and immigration services ombudsman.* Department of Homeland Security. https://www.dhs.gov/sites/default/files/publications/cisomb/cisomb_2017-annual-report-to-congress.pdf

Meissner, D. (2000). INS Commissioner, to Regional Directors, District

Directors, Chief Patrol Agents, and Regional and District Counsel, *Exercising Prosecutorial Discretion*. www.shusterman.com/pdf/prosecutorialdiscretionimmigration1100.pdf

Meissner, D. & Kerwin, D. (2009). *DHS and Immigration: Taking Stock and Correcting Course.*

Myers, J. L., (2007). Homeland Security Assistant Secretary, to All Field Office Directors and All Special Agents in Charge, *Prosecutorial and Custody Discretion.*www.ice.gov/doclib/foia/prosecutorial-discretion/custody-pd.pdf

Obama, B. (2010). *Remarks by the President on Comprehensive Immigration Reform.* TheWhiteHouse.https://obamawhitehouse.archives.gov/realitycheck/the-press-office/remarks-president-comprehensive-immigration-reform

Obama, B. (2014). *Remarks by the President in Address to the Nation on Immigration.* The White House. https://obamawhitehouse.archives.gov/the-press-office/2014/11/20/remarks-President-address-nation-immigration

Obama, B. (2013). *Remarks by the President on Comprehensive Immigration Reform.Speechtranscript*.https://obamawhitehouse.archives.gov/the-press-office/2013/01/29/remarks-president-comprehensive-immigration-reform

Office of the Press Secretary. (2010). *Press Briefing by Press Secretary Gibbs and Secretary of Homeland Security Napolitano.* 8/13/2010. https://obamawhitehouse.archives.gov/the-press-office/2010/08/13/press-briefing-press-secretary-gibbs-and-secretary-homeland-security-nap

Preston, J. (2012). *Romney Dials Back Acceptance of Obama Immigration Program, N.Y. Times.*http://thecaucus.blogs.nytimes.com/2012/10/03/romney-dials-back-acceptance-of-obama-immigration-program/.

Shahshahani, A. ed., (2009). *Terror and isolation in Cobb: How unchecked police power under 287(g) has torn families apart and threatened public safety.* Atlanta: American Civil Liberties Union Foundation of Georgia. www.aclu.org/files/intlhumanrights/immi- grantsrights/asset_upload_file306_41281.pdf

Skrentny, John D. and López, J. L. (2013). *Obama's Immigration Reform: The Triumph of Executive Action.* Indiana Journal of Law and Social Equality: Vol. 2: Iss. 1, Article 3.https://www.repository.law.indiana.edu/ijlse/vol2/iss1/3. https://edition.cnn.com/2013/06/27/politics/immigration/index.html

Silverleib, A. (2013). *Senate passes sweeping immigration bill. CNN.* http://www.cnn.com/2013/06/27/politics/immigration/

Simanski, J. F. (2013). *CBP Border Security report, fiscal year 2014. US Customs and Border Protection.* http://www.dhs.gov/sites/default/files/publications/ois_enforce ment_ar_2013.pdf

Siskin, A. & Haddal, C. C. (2010). *Immigration-related detention: Current legislative issues (CRS Report for Congress, RL32369).* Library of Congress. Congressional Research Service. https://www.hsdl.org/c/view?docid=28938

Slack, M. (2013) *President Obama's four part plan for comprehensive immigration reform.* The White House. https://obamawhitehouse.archives.gov/blog/2013/01/29/president-obamas-four-part-plan-comprehensive-immigration-reform

The White House. (2021). Fact Sheet: *The Biden Administration Blueprint for a Fair, Orderly and Humane Immigration System.* https://www.whitehouse.gov/briefing-room/statements-releases/2021/07/27/fact-sheet-the-biden-administration-blueprint-for-a-fair-orderly-and-humane-immigration-system/

The White House. (2013). *The economic benefits of fixing our broken immigration System.* https://obamawhitehouse.archives.gov/sites/default/files/docs/report.pdf

Tolbert, C. J. (2010). *Mini symposium: Race and the 2008 presidential election.* Political Research Quarterly, 63(4), 860–862. https://doi.org/10.1177/1065912910378991

US Citizenship and Immigration Services Ombudsman. (2017). *Annual Report 2017.* https://www.hsdl.org/c/view?docid=801960

US Customs and Border Protection (2010). *CBP Annual Financial Report Fiscal Year 2010.* https://www.hsdl.org/c/view?docid=691160

US Citizenship and Immigration Services. (2015). *DHS extends eligibility for employment authorization to certain H-4 dependent spouses of H-1B nonimmigrants seeking employment-based lawful permanent residence.* US CitizenshipandImmigrationServices.https://www.uscis.gov/archive/dhs-extends-eligibility-for-employment-authorization-to-certain-h-4-dependent-spouses-of-h-1b

US Department of Homeland Security Press Office. (2013). *Secretary Napolitano announces final rule to support Family Unity During Waiver Process.* https://www.hsdl.org/c/view?docid=727996

US Immigration and Customs Enforcement. (2015). *ICE Enforcement and Removal Operations Report Fiscal Year 2015.*https://www.ice.gov/sites/default/files/documents/Report/2016/fy2015removalStats.pdf

US Immigration and Customs Enforcement. (2010). *ICE strategic plan FY 2010-2014.* https://www.hsdl.org/c/view?docid=22230

US Immigration and Customs Enforcement. (2007). Memorandum from Julie L. Myers, Homeland Security Assistant Secretary, to All Field Office Directors and All Special Agents in Charge. *Prosecutorial and Custody Discretion,* November 7, 2007, www.ice.gov/doclib/foia/prosecutorial-discretion/custody-pd.pdf

US Immigration and Customs Enforcement. (2005). Memorandum from William J. Howard, ICE Principal Legal Advisor, to the Chief Counsels. *Exercising Prosecutorial Discretion to Dismiss Adjustment Cases.* www.ice.gov/doclib/foia/prosecutorial-discretion/pd-dismiss-adjustment-cases.pdf

US Immigration and Customs Enforcement. (2005). Memorandum from William J. Howard, ICE Principal Legal Advisor, to All Office of the Principal Legal Advisor Chief Counsel. *Prosecutorial Discretion*. www.asistahelp.org/documents/resources/DHS_NTA_discretion_7076BC4F57842.pdf

US Immigration and Naturalization Service. (2000). Memorandum from Doris Meissner, INS Commissioner, to Regional Directors, District Directors, Chief Patrol Agents, and Regional and District Counsel. *Exercising Prosecutorial Discretion*. http://www.shusterman.com/pdf/prosecutorialdiscretionimmigration1100.pdf.

US Homeland Security Advisory Council. (2016). *Report of the Subcommittee on Privatized Immigration Detention Facilities.* US Department of Homeland Security. https://www.hsdl.org/c/view?docid=797955

Valdez, I. (2016). *Punishment, race, and the organization of US immigration exclusion.* Political Research Quarterly, 69(4), 640-654. http//www.jstor.org/stable/44018046

Vaughan, J. (2015). *Concerns about the new priority enforcement program.* Center for ImmigrationStudies. https://cis.org/Vaughan/Concerns-About-New-Priority-Enforcement-Program

www.ingramcontent.com/pod-product-compliance
Lightning Source LLC
Chambersburg PA
CBHW051745250726
48659CB00001B/251